AN EYE FOR A DOG

Illustrated Guide to Judging Purebred Dogs

Written and Illustrated by Robert W. Cole

Wenatchee, Washington, U.S.A.

www.dogwisepublishing.com

A MESSAGE FROM THE PUBLISHER

BOB COLE'S LEGACY

Shortly before this book went to press Dogwise Publishing got news that our author, Bob Cole, had died. I had spoken to him just that day about the exact wording of the dedication of the book to his wife Louise Adele. He wanted to be sure it was just right.

Although I never met Bob face to face I came to know him through our work together. It was a privilege and an honor to work with him. He was a gentleman. Throughout the process he was patient, thoughtful and cooperative as we worked together to communicate his work to future generations of dog fanciers. The task of gathering up and combining more than 20 years of material into this book took more than two years and brought us together in the modern way—by phone, fax and email. Bob knew that his work stimulated discussion, even controversy, but he always softened his position as an expert with words to the effect "This is what I would do in this situation. What do you think?"

An Eye for a Dog involved virtually all of our staff. They assisted in reading, editing, scanning and giving us insightful feedback. Barb Steward and Paula Benson gave us an insider's view of what articles would apply most broadly to the world of dogs and dog showing. Larry Woodward tackled the mountain of material and wrangled it into book form, always keeping us focused on the author's message that anyone can improve his ability to evaluate purebred dogs and have fun while doing it! Dave Riggs gave it the final polish as only a professional editor can and Elaine Melnick, Our Index Lady, made sure the reader could locate all the gems of information throughout the book.

An Eye for a Dog is Bob's legacy to the world of dogs and dog showing. It is the legacy of a man who had a passion for dogs and detail and of a man who wasn't afraid to put his thoughts down in writing and line. He was a brave man. He will be missed.

Charlene Woodward, Publisher

TABLE OF CONTENTS

YOU BE THE JUDGE

Do you have "an eye for a dog?" According to old timers, if you have this "eye" you could be placed in a ring with a large class of a breed you had never seen before and not only come up with the best four dogs in order of merit, but also be able to declare in detail how each of the others depart from basic canine balance. Your eye for a dog is enhanced by experience and with this book you will get lots of experience judging many different breeds and taking many different aspects of dog conformation into consideration.

This visual method of assessing dogs is presented in the form of illustrations and illustrated judging scenarios along with explanatory text. Based on such judging considerations as balance, proportions, type, structure, and movement each exercise includes information about the original function of the dog, the breed standard and evolution of the breed over time. In each example you are invited to place classes of various breeds of dogs in order of merit after learning something about the subject from the text. Your awareness of what is involved in the judging process is increased with each graphic presentation. As the author, I will contribute an opinion as to the order of merit of each class, but in the end the final decision is that of the reader. Go ahead! Disagree with me, challenge me, and above all enjoy yourself!

About the Book

An Eye for a Dog brings together more than 20 years of columns I've written for dog magazines entitled "You Be the Judge." Over the years I've had a great many requests from fanciers, exhibitors, handlers, and judges to combine my non breed-specific illustrated studies of the dog into book form. Aside from its entertainment value, this book is intended to enhance your ability to assess a dog's worth stacked and moving; from inside or outside the conformation show ring. In other words it is intended to help develop your "eye for a dog." Portions of these articles have appeared in *Dog News* and *Dogs In Canada* as well as other publications as columns called *You Be The Judge*.

KEY CANINE STRUCTURE AND TERMINOLOGY

Throughout this book references are made to a number of surface and skeletal points. The names of these points and their position are depicted in these outline drawings of a Staffordshire Bull Terrier. This man-made breed is descended from a crossing of the old-style Bulldog and various terriers near the end of the 1700's to produce a smaller, faster fighting dog. His short, smooth, close coat and muscular body allows these important points to be easily seen.

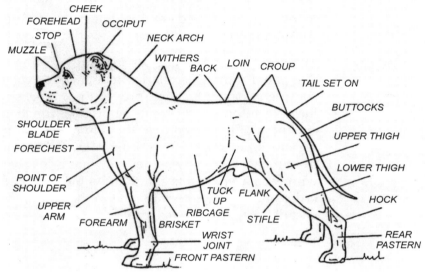

Canine Surface Terminology

All breeds have the same number of bones except in their tails, some being docked. The size, length and position of the bones vary depending on the breed. The dog's outer shape and its action moving is very much dependent on the form these bones take. This drawing will serve as a general reference to skeletal terminology.

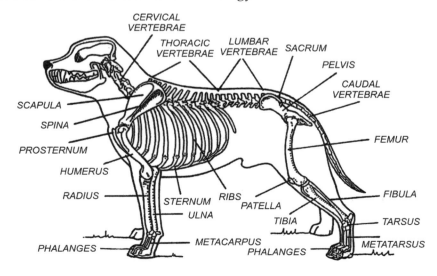

Canine Skeletal Terminology

PART I

TYPE, BALANCE AND PROPORTIONS

CHAPTER ONE
DO YOU HAVE AN EYE FOR A DOG?

The Test

Do you have "an eye for a dog?" According to the old-timers if you have this "eye" you could be placed in a ring of spotless Dalmatians and not only come up with the best dog but be able to declare how each of the others depart from basic Dalmatian balance. There is nothing mystical about having an eye. Artists have this gift, as do millions more who cannot draw but who have an inherent appreciation for volume, space, line, balance, and symmetry. In judging dogs, you need to have formulated an image of "typical", i.e., conformity to the breed Standard in your mind's eye. You also need to have an awareness of the breed's purpose, what it was originally bred to do. Now you're invited to test your eye for a Dalmatian.

The Dalmatian

If you do not have a mental image of a typical Dalmatian allow me to provide one. I have drawn what a Dalmatian looks like both with and without spots. Focus your eye on volume, space, line, balance and symmetry. At this point, head qualities will not be a factor. My typical dog is 23 inches tall. The Dalmatian's neck

Typical Dalmatian with and without spots

is described as "fairly long," the body slightly longer than high (my interpretation of "almost square"). The body is the same depth as the foreleg is long, and the elbow is level with the brisket. It is a dog of many talents, including hunter and shepherd. The Dalmatian is a good representative of the canine norm because, as a coaching dog, he is physically fitted for endurance at a steady trot. He continues gaily on for mile after mile and he does this with strength and ease.

The next illustration depicts a good moving Dalmatian. He moves well because he has good balance. If he departed from typical in terms of balance, the trot would be affected. With this trotting image in mind we would be less likely to accept a short leg or a long body, etc.

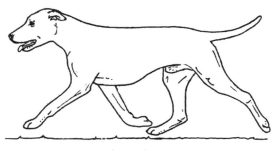

A good mover

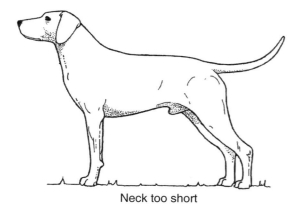
Neck too short

The illustration at left presents in graphic form an appreciation of how little it takes to change physical balance and the surprising effects on the eye these changes produce. With an image of typical in mind, in what way is this spotless Dalmatian not balanced? Answer: His neck is one inch shorter than "fairly long." How much at this scale is one inch? It is one twenty-third of his height or the distance between the top of his skull and the parallel line drawn above it. Not much, but enough to change balance.

The next two examples share a common departure compared to the typical Dalmatian. What is it? To compensate for this departure and to regain a degree of balance (but not Dalmatian balance), two modifications were made to dogs A and B. What are they?

The common departure is that both their bodies are one inch deeper than typical. To regain a degree of balance I increased the size of the head and thickened the "fairly long" neck of Dog B. Balance is improved but this example is now too heavy for an endurance trotter.

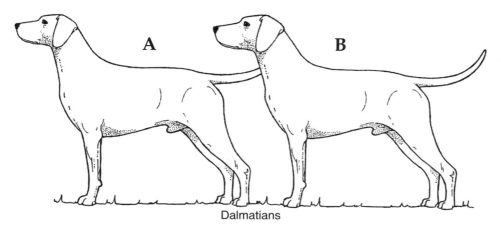
A   B

Dalmatians

Staying with the deeper body, you have probably read the words "solid, standing four-square, balanced" to describe certain substantial breeds like the Bull Terrier. The two dogs shown here are very similar, but Dog C is more solid on his feet. How was this done? Depth or length of body has not changed nor has leg length, but the hind legs are more powerful. In breeds with this more solid balance, the brisket drops down slightly below the elbow — not enough that the forearm curves around the ribcage but sufficient that a more solid stance is produced.

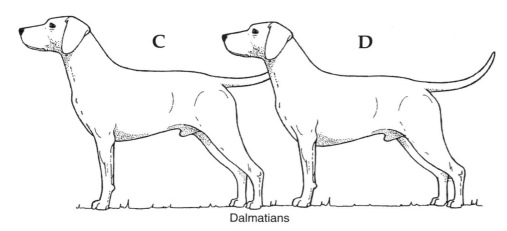
C   D

Dalmatians

3

In such cases, some breed Standards mention this fact, others do not. In terms of proportional balance, this elbow overlap, in reducing height, has returned balance to slightly longer than tall.

This poorly constructed example at right is balanced front with rear because both ends are equally faulty. One end fault doesn't cancel out a fault on the other end, but at least one end doesn't oppose the other. To be truly balanced, a dog must appear to "rest there." This dog makes one feel awkward. Can you identify his many faults? They are: (1) the steep shoulder blade and steep upper arm have forced the body up above the elbow; (2) the withers lack height; (3) the too far forward position of the steep forequarters reduces the forechest and forces the front pasterns to adopt a vertical support; (4) the tail sets on low and the steep hind legs lack desired angulation at both stifle and hock.

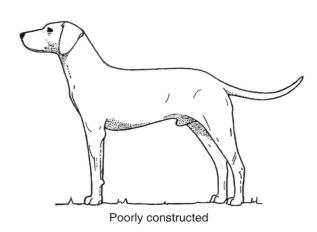
Poorly constructed

The 1989 AKC Dalmatian Standard describes the body as approximately equal in length to height at the withers. In plain English, the typical Dalmatian is slightly longer than tall, but it seems not everyone likes the ratio expressed this way. Our next example, however, is square, and as such does not have the balance of an endurance trotter. Why?

This Dalmatian has the same length of body as the typical example that we began with, but is one inch taller. He is taller because his legs are one inch longer making him square, with long rather than medium length legs. Square brings a danger of foot interference under the body in the show ring at the trot.

Some long-legged Sighthounds are practically square. However, they have specialized fronts that help minimize the danger of foot interference. In comparing the next two examples, is your "eye for a dog" able to recognize the special physical form this minimization of danger from foot interference takes?

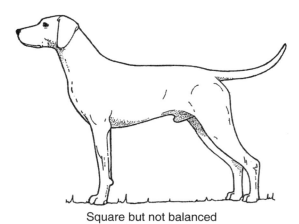
Square but not balanced

You should be aware that Dog E has slightly too long a length of foreleg. Dog F also has too long a length of foreleg, however he has been modified in four ways to resemble a Sighthound more than a white, long-legged Dalmatian. What are these four Sighthound modifications and what

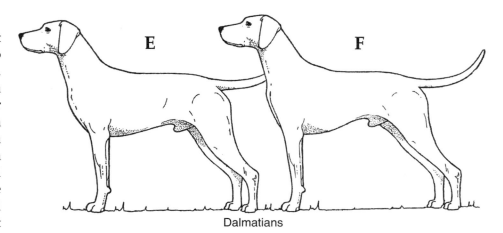
Dalmatians

special changes to the front help minimize foot interference at the trot? (1) The neck is now long rather than fairly long; (2) the increase in tuck-up enables the body to bend to a fuller extent at the fast gallop; (3) a little more length has been given to the second thigh; and (4) the angle between shoulder blade and the upper arm is now more open, bringing the elbow forward on the body, which in turn increases the distance between front and hind legs, thereby reducing the danger of foot interference.

Now let's move on to two more examples. Both of these dogs are — correctly — slightly longer in body than height at the withers but only one has the correct balance for a typical endurance trotting Dalmation. Which one? Your eye should tell you that Dog H is correct and that long-legged Dog G has one inch added to his body length. He is slightly longer than tall but his balance is an obvious departure from typical.

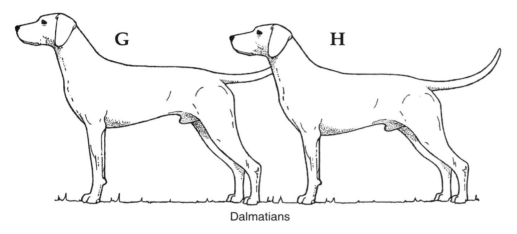

Dalmatians

Your image of typical having been refreshed, you should have little difficulty determining the cause of the next dog's departure from typical. The difference is only one inch but your eye should tell you that he is a little long in the body.

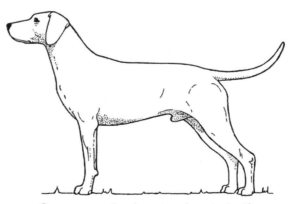

Can you see the departure from typical?

In examining our next dog, we see that this example's proportions resemble more those of a square Boxer or a Doberman Pinscher. He is square but a quite different square than any of the previous examples. Why? Having legs of correct medium length, he is square because his body is one inch shorter.

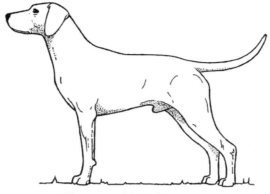

The wrong kind of square

Our last dog below has a final disturbing departure that is perhaps the easiest to recognize for those whose eye is developed. And the most difficult to recognize for those not having an eye for a dog. In spite of this departure, this dog moves well in profile. His legs are one inch shorter than typical. Moved at the same speed as a well-constructed trotting Dalmatian, there would be a space left open under the dog just as if the body was too long. Moved at too fast a trot (the speed where left to his own devices he would break into a gallop), the open or empty space fills in.

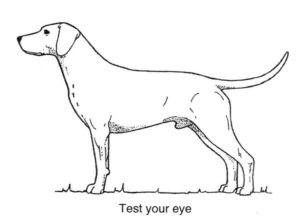

Test your eye

CHAPTER TWO
TYPE

What Is Type?

In judging dogs, type is considered essential. The question then is, "What is type?" Ask 10 judges to define type and you are likely to receive 10 different answers — and they could all be correct. The answers differ because type, as applied to dogs, has a very broad and special meaning. It infers that a set of features listed in the Standard are all-present and in the right proportion. I have two favorites. One is from the late Tom Horner, who wrote, "Type is the sum of those points that make a dog look like its own breed and no other." The other is Edd Bivin's answer. Bivin says in part, "Type is the essence of a breed and may be defined as the picture or image of a breed derived from those characteristics that make the breed different and distinctive from all others. Type characteristics are often overlooked in evaluating dogs but one must remember that without type, the identity of the breed is lost."

So the key is to look like its own breed—but not another. A judge must take into account a large number of features relating to type when evaluating a dog. I have selected several examples and shall attempt to illustrate each, beginning with three American Staffordshire Terriers.

American Staffordshire Terriers

Untypical or Lacking Type?

Which one of these three Am Staffs represent typical and conforms to its breed Standard? Which one is untypical and which one is merely lacking in type? The difference can be subtle depending on degree but not in the case of these three examples. An Am Staff like Dog B that is too lightly built is untypical, lacking bone and substance. A dog that is well built but has a coarse head like Dog C, is said to be is lacking in type. The head need not be coarse to lack type —other variations from typical can cause a dog to lack type as well. This is especially true in breeds that closely resemble each other. The following trio is a good example.

The Staffordshire Bull Terrier is an ancestor of the American Staffordshire Terrier and is somewhat similar in general type, balance, character, and conformation. While size is obviously different, each breed has certain distinctive features that make it a separate entity, especially with regard to the head. Some of the Am Staff's head features are reminiscent of its ancestor and, aside from ears, their Standards are similar. The subtle differences in head type between these two breeds are easier to depict than describe. To show you what I mean I have taken a good head from a Staffordshire Bull Terrier (Dog E) and placed it on the Am Staff but left it with typical Am Staff ears. The resulting type differences between the Am Staff on the left and on the right are subtle but definite. Should this situation occur, is the Am Staff on the right untypical or merely lacking type? Like Dog C in the previous example, I would say he is merely lacking type.

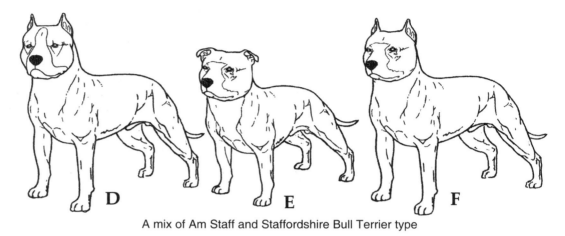

A mix of Am Staff and Staffordshire Bull Terrier type

Type Can Affect Movement

Now let's look at two smooth Dachshunds, stacked and coming. The typical example is Dog A that has a wrap-around digging front where the wrists position closer than the elbows standing. Moving, the wrapped around legs converge under the body. Dog B has straight front legs and short, steep upper arms. Instead of the front legs wrapping around the body and inclining slightly inward, they travel directly forward the same distance apart at the feet as at the elbows. In profile, due to the short upper arms, its reach is limited. Unfortunately, this incorrect Dachshund action coming often has appeal for those who are not familiar with this unorthodox front assembly.

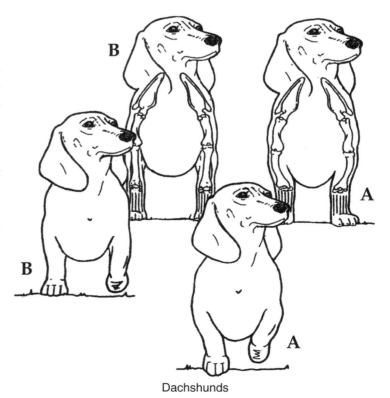

Dachshunds

8

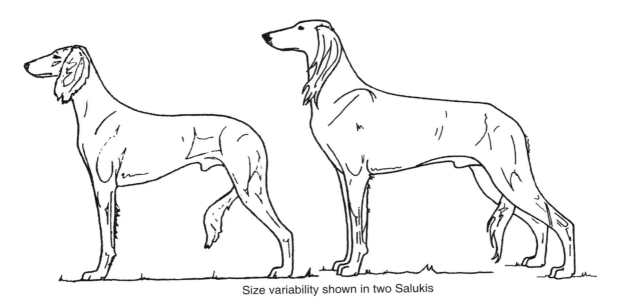
Size variability shown in two Salukis

Versatility and Type

Size, prey, and terrain can influence type, none more so than in the Saluki, a North African Sighthound. This breed's Standard is intentionally vague. It allows the breed to range between 23 and 28 inches, with bitches generally being considerably smaller than males. Breeders believe that more precise wording would produce a generic Saluki limiting versatility as well as this Sighthound's ability to kill gazelle or other quarry over deep sand or rocky mountains. In this breed, big is not necessarily better.

Another type factor governing your choice between these two Salukis relates to their action at the trot. One of these Salukis excels with tremendous reach and drive in the show ring at the trot, the other's action at the trot is less impressive and can best be described as "a light, springy, floating, effortless, energy efficient movement." Many Saluki breeders want you to be aware that long distances on the hunt are covered by the Saluki at the trot not the gallop; therefore action at the trot should appear seemingly effortless, conserving energy for the final fast gallop. Tremendous reach and drive at the trot is not a Saluki requirement.

On the other hand, many judges are of the opinion that the best angulated Saluki, the one that moves around the show ring with tremendous reach and drive, is most likely to also excel at the fast gallop. Both these Salukis have won Specialties. The choice between them is yours. My choice is the smaller, more energy efficient Saluki on the left.

Color and Type

There are even differences in type within a breed based on color. The English Cocker Spaniel is an example. Tom Horner in the English *Dog World*, advises the "solid coloured English Cockers, the blacks, reds and goldens are quite different in type from the blue roans, lemon and whites, and black and whites. They differ in head, in coat, very often in character and in construction; the solid colours are short and compact, the others colours are often more racy and softer in expression."

A Breed With More Than One Type — The Bull Terrier

Some people maintain that a breed has only one type and that type is the one promoted in the Standard. This is not true. Any 10 people reading a breed Standard may have 10 different mental pictures of the dog the Standard describes. This is to be expected. The way standards are written and read, you can be assured there is more than one acceptable type in every breed.

The Bull Terrier serves as a good example of multiple types within a breed because it is a manufactured breed. The balance of bull and terrier sometimes swings in favor of either extreme rather than down the middle of the road. Sometimes it swings intentionally because there are breeders who prefer the bull type and others who prefer the terrier type. As each type contributes to maintaining a balance between bull and terrier, a variety of types can be equally acceptable. The sub-types of the Bull Terrier are named the Bull, the Terrier, the Dalmatian, and the Middle-of-the-Road. Their value in breeding is to ensure that the breed does not swing too far one way.

This illustration shows the Middle-of-the-Road type, a desirable balance between Bulldog and Terrier combining substance and agility. Not all Middle-of-the-Road types are as well balanced as this example. One of the other three sub-types could be superior. If you judged to one particular type and not to the best Bull Terrier you would be doing the breed a disservice. There are four acceptable types in this breed and any one could be better than the other three types on any given day.

Bull Terrier: Middle-of-the-Road type

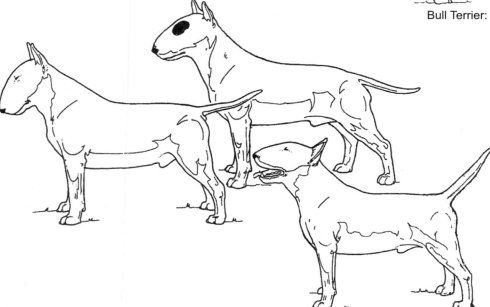

Bull Terrier: Identify the three Bull Terrier types

These three Bull Terriers represent the three other acceptable types. You should not have trouble deciding which is Terrier, which is Bull, and one visually carries traces of the Dalmatian's clean conformation. The Terrier type has a level sacrum that, as on a Fox Terrier, positions its tail too high, but otherwise he is well made. The Bull type has substance and power. The Dalmatian type has elegance and would probably be the best mover. From left to right they are the Bull type, the Dalmatian type, and the Terrier type.

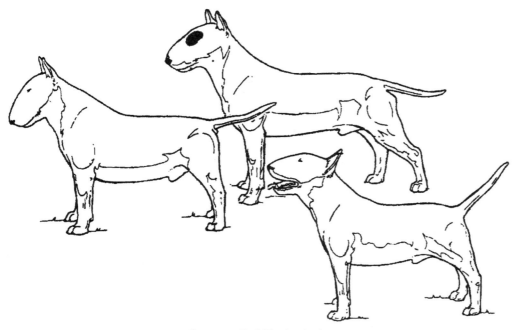

Common Bull Terrier faults

Looking at common faults for each type, the Bull type on the left shows a common departure — that is, short legs. Second would be his steep front and third his steep rear. Notice the lack of forechest and buttock shelf under the tail. The fourth departure — disturbs balance — the head being too small for the heavy body. The Dalmatian type in the center departs toward long legs and long body. Notice that his ears are also set on low. He is, however, well-angulated front and rear. The Terrier type on the right has a short, steep upper arm combined with steep shoulders. Notice that the front pasterns also lack a slight slope. The topline is good but the tail sets on low as well as being carried high. The lack of buttocks balances with the lack of forechest and there is insufficient angulation at stifle and hock.

Another Example — The Border Collie

Is there more than one type in the Border Collie breed? I believe there are a number. However, I am going to focus on just two that have to do with their original sheep herding purpose. One of these two Border Collies is a generic show dog, the other is closer to being a sheep herder and, as you will see, moves like one in the show ring. Stacked, in profile, can you tell which is the generic type and which is the working type? Which do you prefer?

Dog A is the sheep herding example. Dog B, the generic show dog Border Collie, differs only in one feature — the nape of the neck, which greatly changes this breed's balance. Many Border Collie fanciers believe the change is a great improvement, Others are concerned that "stealth" will be lost.

Sheep herding vs. Show Border Collie

Judges should be aware that many Border Collies move in an unusual manner associated with the stealthy crouch it exhibits herding sheep, as shown here. Unless the judge is aware of this unusual form of locomotion, this distinctive crouching action could be a handicap, especially when competing with generic Border Collies that move in a more acceptable fashion.

Stealthy movement

To illustrate what I mean I have produced drawings of two Border Collies moving at the same speed in profile. One moves in the manner of most endurance trotting breeds, reaching full forward and back with all four legs, the topline level, and the head carried high. This appears more normal in the show ring than in the sound, but stealth-like action of the sheep herding dog shown to the right.

Author and judge Anne Hier advises in a handout, "Judges should be aware that many Border Collies move in what might be described as a crouched position. This is typical of the breed and should not be confused with cringing behavior—which denotes incorrect temperament."

By crouched, I believe that Hier means the dog sinks down on itself. I have attempted here to depict this action in contrast to the norm.

Two types of movement

Type vs. Soundness — The Doberman Pinscher

Here is a class of three Doberman Pinschers. This is a class in which you must take structure into consideration as well as proportions. You should be aware that the Doberman Pinscher is a square breed; the same length of body from forechest to buttocks as from withers to ground, so deciding on first place will not be difficult. What will be difficult is deciding on second place.

Dobermans

Dobe C is sound but is long in body. Dobe B is square but lacks forechest, neck arch, shoulder angulation, and angulation at stifle and hock. Which one will you place second? Would you say that even with his structural faults Dobe B is the more typical? How important is square? Which of the two will function best? I placed Dobe C second.

National Types — The German Shepherd

Countries have been known to take and remake a breed in the image they consider currently correct. This can produce a new, distinctive second type within the breed. The German Shepherd is a good example of a current international program to do just that. The German Shepherd on the left is called the Germanic type while the dog to the right is called the Alsatian type. There are other differences, but the most noticeable difference between the two is their toplines. The breed has recently undergone great physical changes in the country of origin. The Germanic type labeled "banana back" by those to whom the result has not met with approval, especially in parts of the world with large followings of the Alsation type. The difference between the two types is so great that it is highly unlikely a specialty judge would be invited to judge both types.

Germanic vs. Alsatian

Italian Greyhound movement

The sound, nicely angulated Whippet—although designed to excel at the fast gallop —moves in the show ring at what is called the "Daisy Clip" where the feet are carried straight forward close to the ground in a graceful fashion. The same cannot be said for this correctly moving Italian Greyhound whose high-stepping action is typical for this toy breed. Both the Whippet and the Italian Greyhound move in a manner typical for their respective breeds. A Whippet that carries its head as high as that of the Italian Greyhound and exhibits high-stepping action would not be typical. The same is true in reverse. However, one Italian Greyhound breeder has volunteered the information that the Whippet's action holds certain appeal for some Italian Greyhound judges. She claims she finishes Italian Greyhounds that move like Whippets three times faster than those that have a high-stepping action.

There is no such thing as a universal trot. A square breed doesn't move in the same manner as a rectangular breed. A German Shepherd doesn't trot in the same manner as a Belgian Malinois nor does the Border Collie move in the same fashion as the Rough Collie. Action differs depending on height, body length, length of leg, angulation, original purpose, size, gait, and attitude. Movement at the trot is very much a part of type.

The Coat

Coat—which includes color, texture and marking—is more important in some breeds than in others. That which is typical for a breed is usually well documented. Of course, skilled presentation can improve a coat of incorrect texture, but the knowledgeable judge should be able to see through the deception, or at least to recognize those specimens with typical texture. But what is typical texture? For instance, the reason you seldom see a Dandie Dinmont Terrier with the required "pily" or "penciled" coat, which is a combination of hardish outer coat and soft undercoat, is because of the state of the art of grooming. Coats are shampooed and the hardish and soft hairs are separated by combing and brushing. Is this separation now the typical Dandie Dinmont coat texture?

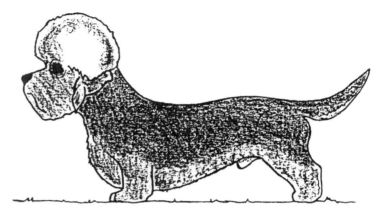

The Dandie Dinmont Terrier

The West Highland White Terrier should be white but the typical hardish coats are often tipped with wheaten. What do you do when the back of the Best in the Class is more yellow than white? And then there is the trimming. Does this Westy represent typical length of leg, proportions, and trim? I believe it could.

The West Highland White Terrier Club of America advises: "Regarding coat texture, we need to stress the double coat and the words hardish, straight, and white. We all want to see impeccably white, hardish coats, but a very hard coat may show some wheaten tipping. When we must, we compromise, just as you must often compromise. Since the Standard gives preference to a hardish, off-white coat over a white fluffy one, we must breed and you must judge accordingly."

The West Highland White Terrier

Be careful not to be taken in by clever trimming. Too low to ground Westies can be trimmed to appear higher stationed. By knowing what to trim and what not to trim, magic can be performed to make a long dog's body shorter, a topline level, and produce the appearance of angulation where little exists. Artifice is to be expected. Not discovering it promotes the belief that it is easier to get a dog to look like a winner than to breed one.

CHAPTER FOUR
INTERNATIONAL BREED VARIETIES

Is there such a breed as an American Brittany? An American Beagle? An American Afghan Hound? How about an American English Springer Spaniel? There clearly are national differences in some breeds, as anyone who has judged overseas will tell you. But, whether or not breeders in countries like the USA have departed from country of origin type to the extent that we should classify their dogs as a separate breed or variety, is subject to debate. The Brittany or the American Brittany is a good example.

The Brittany

Which one of these two Brittanys stacked and moving represents the American Brittany? Dog A represents a European Brittany while Dog B represents the American Brittany. American Brittany breeders have created a hunting, pointing, and retrieving gun dog for show that is so far removed from that of the country o,f origin that it should be rightly named the American Brittany. Not only does the American variety not look like the French variety, they don't work in the field the same way, and their temperament is different.

Americans began importing Brittanys from France in 1931 and continued to do so right up to the beginning of World War II. All were orange and white or liver and white. Black and white had been a disqualification in France since 1908. During World

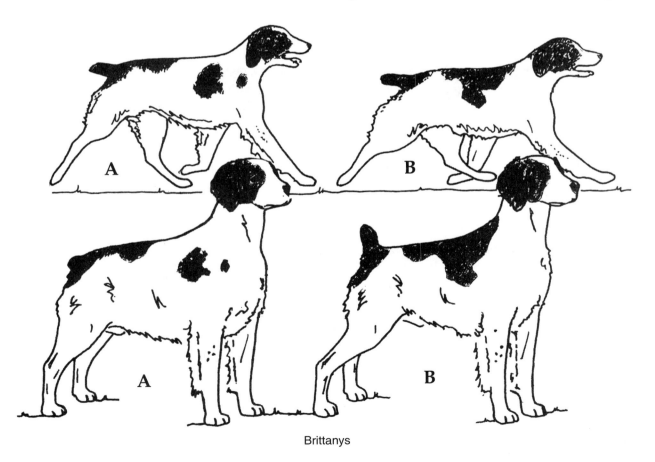

Brittanys

War II, the French endured six years of hardship during which time dog breeding and the feeding of litters had a very low priority. By the end of the war, Brittanys in France were few in number, resulting in a limited gene pool and an increase in the unwanted black color. British and French breeders struggled for 15 years to eliminate this infusion of black but by 1960 they were forced by necessity to recognize black and white as an acceptable color. Black is always a disqualification in the American Brittany.

Then there is the matter of over-reach in profile at the trot. The American variety over-reaches, the European variety does not. The American variety's over-reach is due to a longer length of leg and a shorter body that impacts angulation and speed. Some breeder-judges suggest that this over-reach is correct for the Brittany as long as the dog does not crab. Others have stated that the Brittany should not over-reach at the show ring trot. I leave it to the specialists to sort this out.

The Beagle

Which one of these two Beagles stacked in profile represents an American "type" and which one a British "type"? Both are 15 inches, the maximum for the American Beagle. The maximum for the British Beagles is 16 inches but since height is not one of the two major differences between these two "types" I have drawn them the same size. The two major differences relate to structure/conformation and the resulting action at the trot coming and in profile.

Intentionally similar, there are two structural differences between these two Beagles.

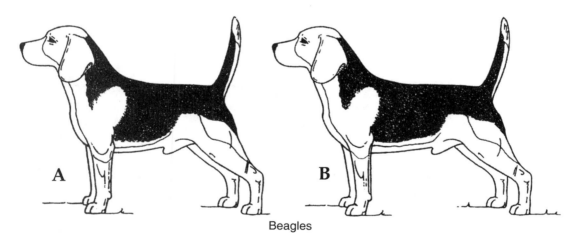

Beagles

Have you determined what these two are? The American Beagle, Dog A, has a much shorter body, the AKC standard asking for a "short back." The British standard asks for a "short coupling", not a short body. The British Beagle, Dog B, is slightly longer than tall, whereas the American Beagle is almost square. The British Beagle has a longer leg, a longer upper arm, and its elbow positions more rearward on the body. Many square American Beagles have a short, steep upper arm, which reduces reach forward and extension rearward of the front leg under the body. These structural differences have a direct influence on how each moves.

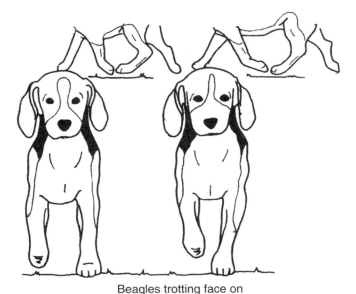

Beagles trotting face on

In the next illustration we have two Beagles trotting face on, the feet turning neither in nor out. Which one is the American and which one British? The feet of the American mover are the same distance apart at the feet as at the elbow due to its short steep upper arm. The British Beagle's forelegs converge slightly. Above their heads I have drawn the major action difference moving in profile, which is the degree the front pastern flexes. This American front pastern hardly flexes. If you think of the front pastern as the minute hand of a clock, the American Beagle flexes to only 5 o'clock. The British front pastern flexes to 4 o'clock (endurance trotting breeds flex to 3 o'clock or 90 degrees).

Many American Beagles have retained a degree of short body combined with moderate angulation and their appearance and action at the trot coming, going, and in profile is a pleasure to watch. These Beagles are not square but neither are they too long.

The Afghan Hound

It is convenient, and probably true, that many of the current differences between American and British Afghans are due to their having been bred to different Standards. At one time in Britain there were two separate Afghan Standards, the Bell Murray and the Ghaznis. In the U.K., the Ghaznis Standard won out but when Americans adopted a Standard in 1926 it was based on the Bell Murray Standard.

There are a few minor differences and one major difference. The British Afghan Standard calls for a "body of moderate length." I interpret moderate as slightly longer than tall, as reflected in the dog on the left. The American Standard describes the body with, "The height at the shoulders equals the distance from the chest to the buttocks." I interpret this description as square, the body the same length as the dog is tall.

Afghan Hounds: British and American

The Labrador Retriever

Based on the 1994 AKC Labrador Retriever Standard, only one of these two examples can be American. Which one? The answer can be found in the 1994 AKC revision that added two important sentences: "Distance from the elbow to the ground should equal half the height at the withers." And: "The brisket should extend to the elbows but not perceptibly deeper."

Note that the British Champion, Dog A, has a chest that drops below the elbow. The resulting stance is both solid and distinctive but not what is looked for in the USA. The American Labrador's elbow is level with his brisket, producing a balance that is quite different. Do you think that is enough difference that the two could be thought of as two Labrador Retriever varieties?

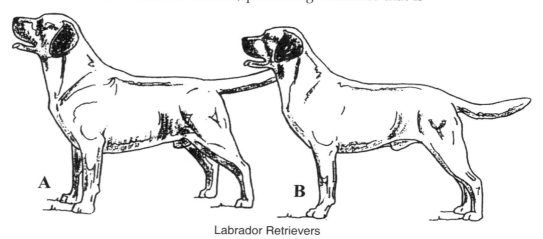

Labrador Retrievers

The English Springer Spaniel

Which one of these two English Springer Spaniels is American? Is she sufficiently different from the British dog that you would class them as separate breeds?

In England, the English Springer Club members present at the February 1993 annual general meeting unanimously agreed that the majority of Springers shown in America should no longer be classified as English Springer Spaniels as they do not comply with the breed Standard as laid down by the country of origin. The chairman, Janet Wood, has written to the AKC, the KC, and the FCI suggesting a split in the breed similar to

English Springer Spaniels

the English-American Cocker Spaniel division. In her letter to national kennel clubs, Wood advised that "it is of particular concern to us that these flashy, untypical dogs are being exported in increasing numbers to European and Scandinavian countries and will ruin the true breed type there."

Many North Americans disagree. They claim it is not departure from "true breed type" that these "flashy" American exports to Europe represent. They would claim that it is a departure from centuries old showdog style and presentation. They argue that American Springers do conform to the breed Standard as laid down by the country of origin. My drawings point out that the so-called over-groomed American Springer Spaniel, Dog B, does not conform to the English take-me-as-I-am way of presenting the breed. The difference between the two is not conformation; the difference is merely one of presentation.

The Siberian Husky

The next British-American breed comparison is different than the above example because it is the British who have created a new variety. The breed is the Siberian Husky. I do not think you had trouble identifying Sibe B as the new variety. The British example I chose is a fast, short-distance runner as well as a show winner of two Reserve CCs. He doesn't conform to the original requirement to pull a sled over snow-covered terrain for long distances. Snow and long distance aren't possible in the U.K., so the sleds have wheels and the distance is short.

The present trend for breeding fast-running dogs over relatively short distances is commendable as part of a successful effort to retain the breed's working ability, desire to run, team spirit, and correct temperament. At the same time, be aware that this form of sprint racing does not promote some of the qualities the original dogs were bred for. Be that as it may, in addition to producing some of the world's best Siberians, the British have now produced a distinct "sprint" variety that affords racing pleasure in situations where there is little or no snow.

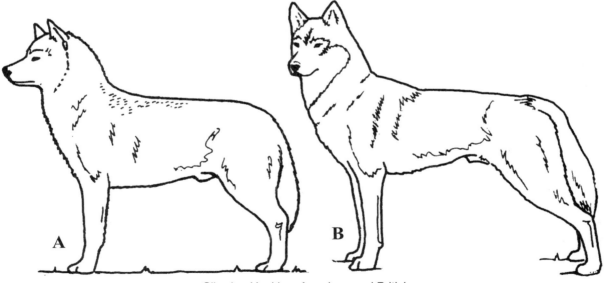

Siberian Huskies: American and British

CHAPTER FIVE
IMPROVING DRAWINGS

Sometimes a drawing of mine representing a particular breed of dog is not satisfactory. When this happens, I often turn to breed experts for assistance. With their help I usually have been able to improve on the drawings in question. The improvements are often subtle but important. This improvement process is a great visual learning experience for me, and I hope, you.

Selected for your consideration are "before" and "after" drawings of different breeds in need of improving, some requiring several modifications. You are invited to decide what features need improvement and see the end results.

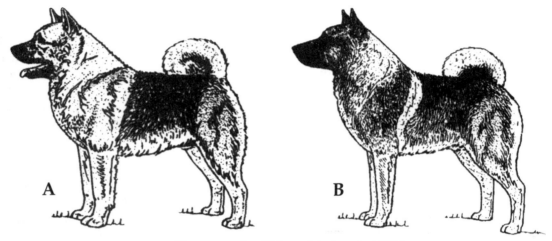

The Norwegian Elkhound: before and after

The Norwegian Elkhound

Much of the quality of the drawings are dependent on the availability of published technical information that goes beyond the wording in a breed Standard and input from knowledgeable breeders. Some breeders, like Karen B. Elvin of Sangrud Norwegian Elkhound fame, have the exceptional ability of being able to graphically suggest improvements with a red pen as opposed to well intended but vague wording. The end result is often very satisfactory, as in the case of the Norwegian Elkhound. This happy relationship between breeder and illustrator reveals some of the detail that is involved in depicting type.

My original drawing of Dog A closely resembles a real-life Elkhound champion. It was suggested by Elvin that there were several ways that this dog could be improved. To improve on Elkhound Champion A, the following modifications to Dog B were made: (1) the muzzle is now the same length as skull; (2) the eye is enlarged slightly and moved up higher in skull, the stop defined in part by the eyebrows; (3) he has tight lips (Elkhounds do not have flews); (4) the gray body is now darkest on the saddle and the tip of tail is black and protrudes to one side, (the bone of the tail actually kinks at the end and cannot be unrolled); (5) the angle of the croup now complements (follows) pelvis slope (sacrum was incorrectly depicted as horizontal); and (6) the distinctive lighter color harness mark (a band of longer guard hairs from shoulder to elbow) is now a little farther back.

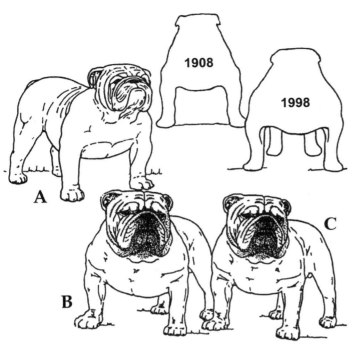

A

B

C

Bulldog fronts: Dog A; Dog B; Dog C

The Bulldog

Sometimes, when there is a difference of opinion, a single feature will require that two drawings represent typical. The Bulldog's wide front is a good example; experts remain at odds. Bulldog A was part of an article reproduced years ago as a training aid by the Bulldog Club of America. One of the educational spin-offs not mentioned in the article but raised as a question later, dealt with the shape of the space between the Bulldog's front legs. Was the space to be depicted as rectangle (Dog B) or square (Dog C)? Eight years later the question is still asked. Which drawing do you believe is the more correct?

I believe that Dog C, whose forelegs form a square, is the more correct Bulldog front. The outline front, dated 1908, is a trace from the book *The Perfect Bulldog* by J. Hay Hutchinson published early in the 20th century that promoted a rectangular front nearly a century ago. This makes the outline old but not necessarily right. By contrast, Dog C's front is based on the square front promoted by *The Bulldog Club of America 1996, Illustrated Guide*. Aside from North America, how does the rest of the world view Bulldog fronts, square or rectangular? There appears to be a preference in some places for the rectangle. Has the clearly rectangular Bulldog front (dated 1998) traced from the cover of the New Zealand Kennel Gazette (September 1, 1998) Breed Supplement met with approval of the Club? Personally I do not believe it has. But it does remind us that the rectangle still has appeal.

The Staffordshire Bull Terrier

You were introduced earlier to the Staffordshire Bull Terrier and four features were discussed. Your task now is to apply this experience by suggesting ways in which a drawing of a Staff can be improved. It was thought that sound Staffordshire Bull Terrier A could serve to represent typical. He had done very well under both all-round judges and specialists, however there were five improvements suggested by Steve Eltinge, a noted Staff breeder. What are they? Compared to our improved drawing B, my first Staffordshire Bull Terrier drawing can be seen to have needed several improvements: (1) the skull needed to be reshaped; (2) the front of the neck needed to be cleaned up; (3) the nape of the neck was made to flow smoothly into withers and then into the back; (4) the loin needed shortening; and (5) tuck-up needed to be increased.

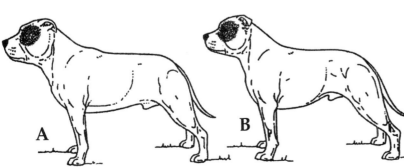

Staffordshire Bull Terrier: before and after

CHAPTER SIX
WHAT IS A TRAD?

One of my articles in *Dog News* met with some concerned response from Saluki breeders. Concerned because, in depicting a certain big winning Saluki, I ended up promoting a TRAD. Do you know what a TRAD is?

A TRAD is a Saluki with "Tremendous Reach And Drive" similar to the dog stacked and moving in profile at the trot. "Well," you might ask, "what is wrong with that?" According to concerned Saluki breeders, the Saluki is not required to exhibit tremendous reach and drive at the trot. The Saluki must travel long distances at the trot over difficult terrain in an energy-conserving manner prepared always to break into a fast gallop. Exhibiting tremendous reach and drive at the trot in the show ring is believed by some to produce only dramatic appeal.

Judges who award TRADs with Group and Best in Show are of a different opinion. Many believe that the best-angulated Saluki, the one that moves with tremendous reach and drive at the trot, is most likely to also excel at the fast gallop. They believe this is as true for the Saluki as it is for a number of non-Sighthound breeds. For those judges, TRADs that were faster, more angulated and more powerful were the contenders for Best of Breed.

A TRAD – stacked and moving

A Comparison

The American champion, Dog A , shown in the next illustration is such a contender. As a TRAD he is impressive, however he lacks certain qualities that some Saluki owners aim for. He departs physically in four ways from correct type. Determine what these four departures from type are.

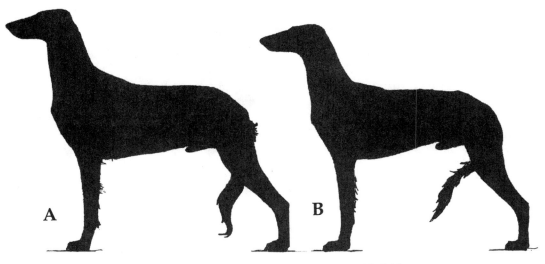

A TRAD vs. a typical Saluki

The TRAD shown is too heavy overall, has the wrong topline, wrong line under the body, and has too long a second thigh. Type is affected — does it really look like a Saluki? The acid test is that, if viewed in silhouette, would it immediately be identifiable as a good Saluki? Presented to many Saluki breeders, he failed the test.

To represent typical I chose again the winner of a Saluki specialty, Dog B. He is lighter, more elegant and he seemed to fulfill the Standards requirement for "the impression of grace and symmetry and of great speed and endurance coupled with strength and activity to enable it to kill gazelle or other quarry over deep sand or rocky mountains." However, once again, some Saluki breeders were not impressed with this example.

Improvements

In order to find a more acceptable example I asked for and received a large judge's information package from Sue Rooney-Flynn, Judge's Education Chair. The information package contained many photographs together with Rooney-Flynn's comments, the intent being that I look beyond the impressive but generic forms of TRAD. Gradually I began to get a feel for a Saluki type that exemplified the word "moderation." I had dozens of examples to choose from, each possessing various levels of moderation, mostly standing in a relaxed pose. However, it was necessary for the purpose of comparison, to depict typical in a formal stack at the angle a judge would make his or her assessment: first in silhouette, then in line. To do so would require improving on reality so I turned first to depicting typical in a relaxed pose . This Saluki met with approval along with some interesting observations. It was noticed that the lowering of the neck could make the muscles over the withers more prominent. The stepping forward of one foot slightly under the dog and the other rear leg extended rearward, makes the not quite perpendicular rear pasterns appear to be slightly long.

This in turn can give the appearance of a more angulated hind leg. Appearances can be deceiving, and for this more than any other reason, I wanted a formal pose.

Flushed with producing a satisfactory "relaxed" pose, I then produced the silhouette shown here and a line drawing shown below. Both fortunately met with the Judge coordinator's approval. They represent typical but not ideal. Ideal would have to go to an official committee to resolve many questions, such as ears. Some ears are set at eye level, some are set higher (I prefer them high). I also prefer head planes that are almost parallel, a flat backskull, a muzzle as long or slightly longer than the skull, tight lips that leave the underjaw exposed, eyes that are set obliquely giving an oriental expression, and, as football players facing the sun know, to protect a desert animal's eyes from the sun, they require dark eye rims fully pigmented.

A Best in Show Saluki in silhouette

You have your preferences and I have mine because these seven unofficial features are not described in the breed Standard. The Saluki Standard is recognized as being a vague guideline and many breeders would have it remain so rather than open the door to change and the promotion of a "Generic Saluki."

Acceptance

These depictions of typical are unlikely to meet with the approval of everyone. Many factors have combined to produce this breed's diversity. This is a breed where there are two coat varieties, a latitude of up to five inches in size, the capability of hunting gazelle or other quarry over deep sand or rocky mountains, and, in addition, there are

A Best in Show Saluki line drawing

geographical differences as well as recognized strains. Many Saluki breeders wish to retain this diversity and to do so they promote moderation and what can be described as "a light, springy, floating, effortless, energy-efficient movement" infrequently seen in Salukis today.

Saluki breeders are not alone in wanting to avoid tremendous reach and failing to see it happen. The classic example of failure to trot in a manner correct for the breed is the Chow Chow. Some Chow Chows move more freely and with more reach and drive than many Samoyed. The Saluki Standard emphasizes the word "moderate" four times but doesn't apply it to gait. For this and other reasons the Saluki Club of America has, among other publications, produced a booklet titled *Judging Salukis* in which the club advises that Salukis "should have a proud bearing, be lithe, quick, graceful, and elegant, be harmoniously proportioned and moderate, and that action at the trot be naturally balanced, smart and free. The Saluki should move with power, grace, and style."

Illustrated Sequences One and Two

It must be remembered that long distances on the hunt are covered by the Saluki at the trot, not the gallop, therefore action at the trot should appear seemingly effortless, conserving energy for the final fast gallop. Not wanted is a Saluki with tremendous reach and drive as depicted in Illustrated Sequence One. What is wanted is a Saluki with moderate reach and extension as is depicted stacked and moving in Illustrated Sequence Two on the next page. Comparisons can be made frame-by-frame, phase-by-phase because the half cycle sequences each begin in Phase 1 with the right front leg in vertical support. From that first frame on, the other three leg positions can vary depending on each dog's individual conformation. The most noticeable overall difference is the greater amount of reach and extension exhibited by the TRAD. Notice

Illustrated Sequence One: TRAD Saluki movement

that the TRAD's right front wrist in Phase 6 is flexed horizontal. By contrast, the correct Saluki in Sequence Two displays a wrist that is more open in Phase 6 denoting the ownership of a more open Sighthound upper arm and travels at a more moderate rate of speed. The TRAD has been trained to not break into a gallop but to continue to trot at a fair rate of speed. Such fast and dramatic action can have great appeal. The action of the "typical" mover is less dramatic but more balanced, effortless, and energy efficient

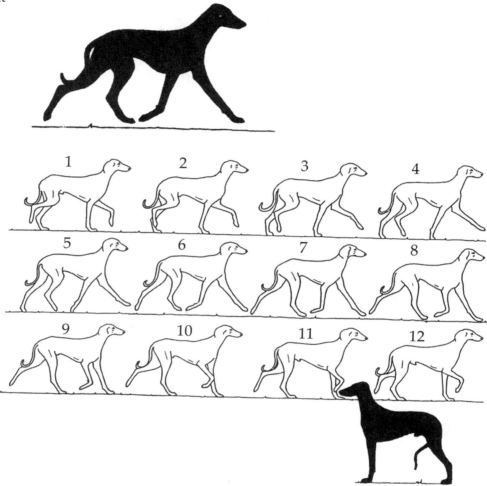

Illustrated Sequence Two: Correct Saluki movement

A

B

Terriers in silhouette

CHAPTER SEVEN
PROPORTIONS

Correct proportions produce distinctive silhouettes. These two terriers appear quite similar, however, slight differences in proportions set them apart. What two terrier breeds are they? Right, one is a Lakeland Terrier and one is a Welsh Terrier — but which is which? The Welsh Terrier B is a heavier breed than the Lakeland Terrier A. Proportions differ only slightly but sufficient to set them apart as separate breeds as shown in the first two illustrations.

Dogs also differ in proportions within their respective breeds due, as in the case of the next eight examples, to depth of body and length of leg. In this chapter you will be presented with eight breeds, two examples in each breed. One example is correctly proportioned and the other is not. All 16 examples are structurally sound. You are invited to judge each pair and select the one dog correctly proportioned for its breed.

Departure from correct proportions can take many directions but in this challenge, departure will be limited to leg length and body depth. Each breed was selected with these two directions in mind and each for a different reason. Sometimes this reason related to breed purpose.

Being able to recognize correct length of leg and depth of body for each breed is an extremely important requirement for judging dogs. Recognition of correct proportions takes into consideration breed type, balance, purpose, and movement at the trot and gallop.

A

B

Lakeland Terrier and Welsh Terrier

The Dalmatian

The Dalmatian is an endurance trotter and the proportions possessed by one of these two dogs reflect this ability. Both have the same length and depth of body. One has correct foreleg length, the other does not. Which example best represents this breed? To excel at the

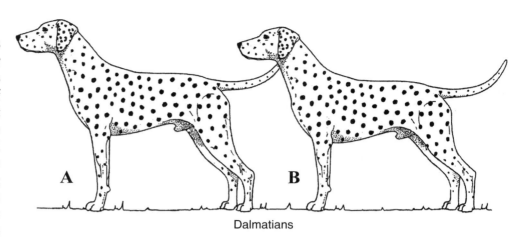

Dalmatians

endurance trot, the body from forechest to buttocks should be slightly longer than height at the withers. The foreleg length should be moderate, i.e., the same distance from elbow to ground as the body measures from withers to distance between withers and ground. Dalmatian B has moderate length of foreleg that fulfills these requirements. Dalmatian A has a long foreleg in ratio to his depth of body. Forelegs come in six lengths: long, moderately long, moderate, moderately short, and short.

The Great Dane

The Great Dane is a breed that should show a square outline. Shown in outline, these two square Great Danes are the same height. The difference between the two is length of leg and depth of body. The Great Dane is not designed for endurance at the trot, his size and weight is more conducive to security.

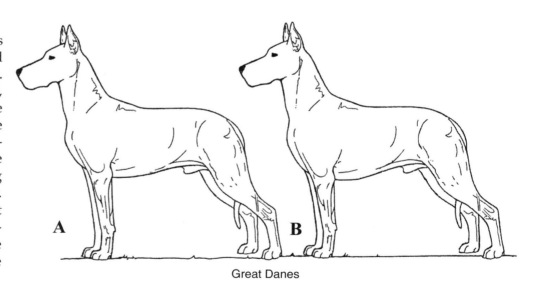

Great Danes

The 1976 AKC Great Dane Standard provided a more detailed direction than most breed guidelines, however it was silent in regard to foreleg length and thus either of the two examples shown could have served to represent correct leg length. In 1990 the AKC Standard was revised and the question of Great Dane foreleg length was addressed. It was resolved in 1990, that to be correctly proportioned, the foreleg must be the same length as the body was deep. This was expressed in this manner: "The elbow should be one-half the distance from the withers to the ground." One sentence, but one that now leaves no doubt that Dane A is the one that is correctly proportioned.

Beagles

The Beagle

These two Beagles are the same height, body length and body depth—in fact they are alike except for leg length and position of elbow. They are the same height despite one having long legs because the elbow of the longer legged Beagle positions one inch *above* the brisket.

The norm is an elbow level with the brisket. The AKC Standard describes the Beagle's foreleg as "straight." The British Standard in addition to "straight" advises that "the chest is let down below elbow," and "height to elbow about half height at withers." Beagle B fulfills the British requirement for a longer foreleg. Since the AKC Standard is silent on foreleg length you can choose either A or B as correct. I would choose B.

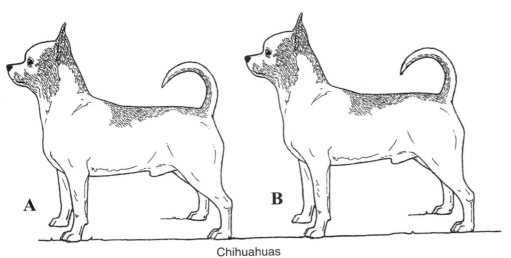

Chihuahuas

The Chihuahua

While there are correct leg and body depth proportions for each of the Toy breeds, the description of foreleg is usually limited to "straight" as we find in the Chihuahua Standard. All Chihuahua Standards describe the breed as slightly longer than tall, however, the 1972 AKC wording expands on this description in a strange way that could influence your choice. The AKC-worded blueprint added: "shorter backs desired in males." I know this doesn't mean at the expense of a longer loin, and that "back" is probably intended to indicate the complete topline, however, be that as it may, this addition suggests a desire that males be closer to square in outline.

Chihuahua A has a moderately short foreleg, shorter in length than depth of body, and a body rectangular in outline. Chihuahua B has a moderate length of foreleg and is square in outline.

Chihuahua B is closer to square; his body relative to height is visually shorter because his longer legs make him taller. Both weigh less than six pounds and as height is not designated, based on the AKC wording, either dog might be taken for correct. In my opinion only one has correct proportions and that one is Chihuahua A.

The Borzoi

These two Borzoi differ in only one respect — the forearms between elbow and wrist are longer on one Borzoi example than on the other. The 1972 AKC Standard doesn't advise as to forearm or foreleg length, but it does

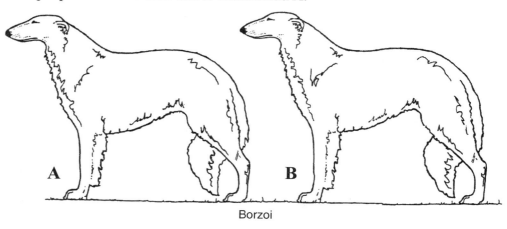

Borzoi

advise that the Borzoi "was originally bred for the coursing of wild game, relying on sight more than scent." In other words, a Sighthound.

Sighthounds require long forelegs to enable them to excel at the fast double-suspension gallop. A foreleg of only moderate length would reduce this ability. The Canadian and British Standards in their latest revisions promote a long foreleg with the words "length of forearm nearly equal to half the total height at withers" plus "a slightly sloping pastern." The two parts, forearm and pastern, combine to produce a long foreleg. My choice for correct is Borzoi B.

You should be aware that not all American Borzoi breeders are in favor of a long leg. Some prefer a moderate length of leg conducive to endurance at the trot, but still long enough to excel at the fast gallop when the need for speed arises.

The Rhodesian Ridgeback

One of these two Rhodesian Ridgebacks is taller than the other because his foreleg is longer. Both are proportionally slightly longer in body than height at the withers, regardless of the difference in height. The shorter legged of

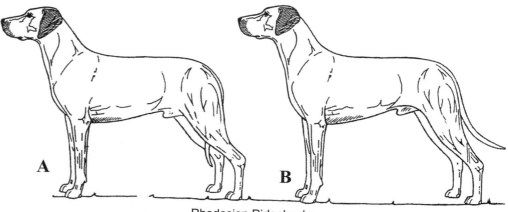

Rhodesian Ridgebacks

the two (moderate length) is capable of the present requirement for "great endurance with a fair amount of speed." The taller is capable of faster speed.

Ridgeback A has a foreleg of moderate length, the same length as depth of body. This length is sufficient to provide both endurance and a fair amount of speed at-the-gallop, the key word being "fair." Greater speed than fair requires greater than moderate length of foreleg.

The American trend (although not ALL Ridgeback fanciers are in favor of "faster is better") towards Ridgeback B's long foreleg, intentionally or unintentionally, is due to the recent acceptance of the Ridgeback as a competitor in AKC Sighthound field trials. Fast speed at the gallop being a major factor in Sighthound trials, a longer leg naturally places the Rhodesian in a more competitive position. Next will be the lightening of the present requirement "legs — heavy in bone." Given a choice, I am staying with Rhodesian Ridgeback A.

The Greater Swiss Mountain Dog

Given AKC Working Group designation in 1994, the Greater Swiss Mountain Dog is the largest and oldest of the four sennenhund breeds developed in Switzerland. Only one of these two Mountain Dogs examples is correctly proportioned for this working breed. Which one?

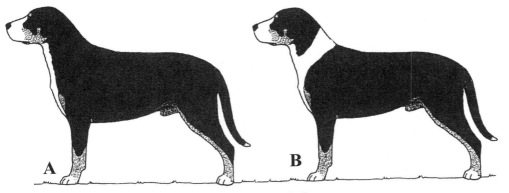

Greater Swiss Mountain Dogs

Both dogs have the same body length and foreleg length but only one has the required 10:9 body length-to-height proportion. To not make this difference in length-to-height ratio immediately apparent, I gave one dog a permitted white collar. The forelegs on A and B are the same length. However in ratio to different body depths, A's length of foreleg is technically "moderately short" while B has a "moderate" length of foreleg. A's body is "full" and the chest is deeper than the foreleg is long. B's foreleg is the same length as the lighter body is deep. A is correct; B's body requires more distance between withers and brisket for a Greater Swiss Mountain Dog.

The Siberian Husky

These two Huskies are similar in all respects except for one important feature relating to sled-dog ability. I would be remiss if I did not take this opportunity to include this major breeder concern. The concern is for a situation where (like one of these two dogs) a very well-angulated, beautiful moving, ground-covering Siberian Husky wins in the show ring but would not be selected to pull a sled.

The example that would not be selected to pull a sled is short on leg for a Siberian Husky. That examples like Siberian Husky B often win in good competition is especially disturbing because, since 1971, the AKC Standards have been emphatic that "length of foreleg from elbow to ground is slightly more than the distance from the elbow to the top of the wither" as displayed by Siberian Husky A.

Siberian Huskies

CHAPTER EIGHT
FEATURES THAT INFLUENCE PROPORTIONS

A discussion of features that influence canine proportions opens the door to an appreciation of a wide variety of breeds and their conformation. Each breed possesses certain features that enable it to excel at the task for which it was intended.

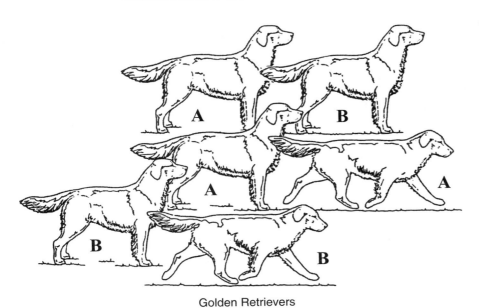

Golden Retrievers

The Golden Retriever

Some breed Standards spell out exactly how long the body should be. The Golden Retriever is a classic example: "Body length measured from the breastbone to the point of buttocks is slightly greater than the height at the withers in a ratio of 12:11." Both of these 24-inch Goldens possess the same degree of angulation front and rear, but differ in length of body. Which one is correct?

Length of body can influence the ability of the Golden to excel at the trot. Trotting at the same speed, Dog B's right rear foot will pass under the flexed right front foot and occupy the spot the right front foot just vacated. Such a trotting motion helps sustain endurance. Dog A's right rear foot will not reach forward enough to step under the right front foot and occupy the spot the front foot just vacated. Dog A's hind foot cannot do so because his body is too long. Another reason might be insufficient angulation at the front, rear, or both. Too often what goes on under the dog trotting in profile is overlooked.

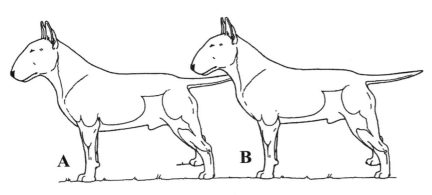

Bull Terriers

The Bull Terrier

There is nothing in the AKC Bull Terrier Standard that says the elbow should position slightly above the bottom of the brisket or that the brisket should drop down lower than the elbow. The Standard does say that the foreleg is of moderate length as is the case for both Dog A and B. It also says that there should be great depth from withers to brisket and that the dog must stand firmly on perfectly straight legs. Both dogs meet those criteria, Dog A perhaps a little more closely because of his low gravity whereas the elbows on Dog B are level with the bottom of the chest. Which one of these Bull Terriers should be favored?

Breeders think of the Bull Terrier as standing four square, untippable, and solid. They usually prefer Dog A's solid stance to that of Dog B. The overlap of elbow and brisket is slight but the effect on balance and proportions is striking.

The Ibizan Hound

The feature that sets the Ibizan Hound apart and influences proportions is the position of his elbow. The chest is deep and long with the breastbone sharply angled and prominent. The brisket is approximately 2½ inches above the elbow and in front of the deepest part of the chest. The shoulder blade is moderately laid-back and joins a rather upright upper arm, the latter's steepness greatly influencing the position of the elbow. The effect is somewhat strange but this breed's speed and jumping ability is well documented.

Ibizan Hound

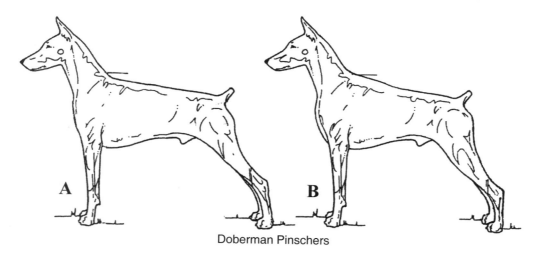

A   B

Doberman Pinschers

The Doberman Pinscher

The height of the Doberman Pinscher's withers can change the ratio of body length to height. Less well-constructed Dog A appears longer in body than Dog B because of low withers. The Standard reads "Height measured vertically from the ground to the highest point of the withers, equaling the length measured from the point of forechest to the rear projection of the upper thigh." The Standard goes on to describe the Doberman's withers as pronounced. The Standard does not inform as to how long the foreleg should be, however I have been told that with good high withers, the foreleg will be as long from elbow to foot as the body is deep from withers to brisket.

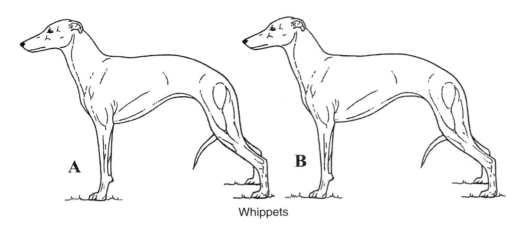

Whippets

The Whippet

There are two schools of thought as to how long the Whippet's body should be in ratio to height. To satisfy both schools the AKC Standard now reads, "Length from forechest to buttocks equal to or slightly greater than height at the withers." Bitch A and Bitch B represent these two official length-to-height ratios. Do you have a preference for one over the other?

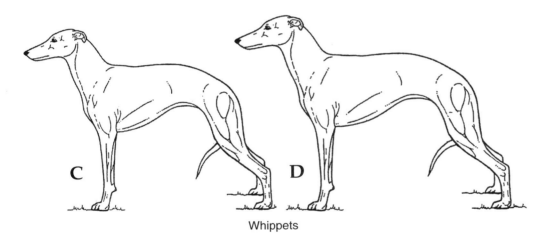

Whippets

It would be easier to make comparison decisions if Whippets were all the same size. In Whippets, size is more a factor in the influence of proportions than a feature. Bitch C stands 18 inches, Bitch D stands the maximum 21 inches (more than a half inch over or under these heights disqualifies). Is Bitch C a scaled-down version of larger Bitch D or is she a scaled-down version of shorter bodied Bitch A? She is a scaled-down version of Bitch A.

The Weimaraner

The Weimaraner's distinctive chest should be well-developed and deep. A forechest less than "well developed" would influence proportions. Dog A lacks forechest because his steep forequarters have moved forward on the body covering the forechest and creating a hole between the front legs. Note that the body has been forced up above the elbow and that the topline lacks the smooth transition from neck into withers. Dog B would be my pick between the two.

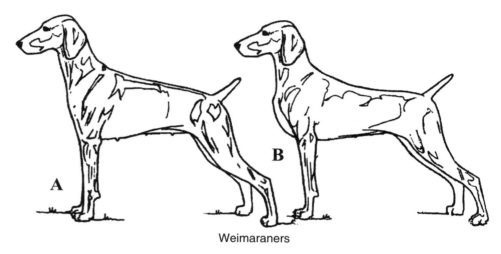

Weimaraners

CHAPTER NINE
CANINE BALANCE

The training of the eye to see balance is a crucial part of being capable of properly evaluating dogs. There are judges who maintain that seeing balance is an innate gift. I am not one of them. I believe if you know the function of the breed, understand why it is built the way it is, have a correct image of ideal in your mind's eye, how it should move and what it takes to move that way, seeing and assessing balance should not be a problem. Simply put, a balanced dog "rests there." Unbalanced dogs produce discord and make you feel uncomfortable.

Irish Setter

I do not think I have ever seen a better description of balance than in the American Breed Standard for the Irish Setter: "The correct specimen exhibits balance whether standing or in motion. Each part flows and fits smoothly into its neighboring parts without calling attention to itself." This quote presents a word picture of a dog that is admirable as a complete whole. This illustration is of a well balanced Irish Setter.

Balance Can Evolve – Norwich vs. Norfolk Terrier

Few breeds have remained completely unchanged in the past half century. Some like the Bull Terrier have changed (downface) via exaggeration. Some, like the Norfolk Terrier A and the Norwich Terrier B, acquired a different balance after they were divided into two separate breeds. Initially, the only difference was that one had drop ears and the other prick ears. After the separation, very gradually but inexorably, the two breeds grew apart until their balance is recognizably different.

They are both still small, red or black and tan or grizzle-colored, low to the ground, feisty little terriers, however the Norfolk is longer in body than the Norwich. Because of body length, the Norfolk is the better mover. Some Norwich are becoming a bit too short bodied and a bit too stocky to be of much use underground but this has not lessened their appeal.

Norfolk Terrier and Norwich Terrier

Balance and the Staffordshire Bull Terrier

Not a great deal of study has been conducted on Staffordshire Bull Terrier balance because exhibitors like to have their dogs photographed at a three-quarter angle. However it is in profile that they are judged and it is in profile that the differences in balance between these two dogs can be appreciated. By himself, Dog A is a worthy contender but compared to Dog B there are eight ways in profile that his balance can be improved. Can you spot them?

Staffordshire Bull Terriers

Now in profile, we can see several ways to improve Dog A. They are: 1) make the head smaller; 2) reshape the forehead; 3) take away the loose skin on the neck; 4) improve the transition of neck into withers; 5) lengthen the legs slightly; 6) make slight changes to loin and croup; 7) increase tuck-up; and 8) give the hindquarters more power.

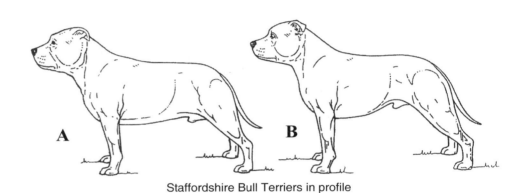

Staffordshire Bull Terriers in profile

Akita A or B?

My dictionary describes balance as "harmony of design and proportion" and, "an even distribution of weight." This is true of canine balance. I shall depend heavily on drawings to convey the meaning of the word balance in many of its different applications as they apply to the judging of dogs, beginning with Akitas.

Akitas

These two Akitas are identical with the exception of one feature. That one feature greatly affects balance and type; the two going hand in hand. You have two decisions to make: 1) What feature is responsible for the difference in balance between these two Akitas? 2) Which balance is correct for this working breed?

44

Applied to individual breeds such as the Akita the word "balance" must be considered in relation to its breed Standard. The Akita Standard reads, "Neck thick and muscular, comparatively short, widening gradually toward shoulders. A pronounced crest blends in with the base of the skull." Dog B has the correct Akita neck length. Dog A's neck is only one inch longer. It is surprising how one inch on a 27-inch tall dog can change balance so much.

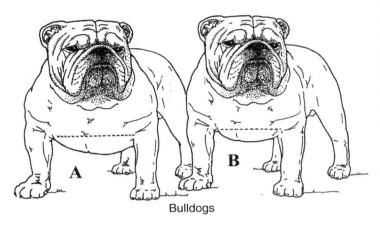

Bulldogs

Bulldog A or B?

Which Bulldog has the correct front? A basic question not answered in the breed Standard. Not all features are described in official breed Standards. Often other sources must be uncovered in order to be sure which of these two Bulldogs is correctly balanced. *The Bulldog Club of America 1996, Illustrated Guide*, a small pamphlet published by the Bulldog Club of America, informs, "Correct turn of shoulder with proper front legs showing straight perpendicular inner forelegs will form a near square." Dog B's front is correctly square. Dog A's obvious rectangle between the front legs indicate that the legs are too short or shoulders are too wide or both. In my opinion, awareness that a square front is the correct balanced front is essential in the judging of this unorthodox breed.

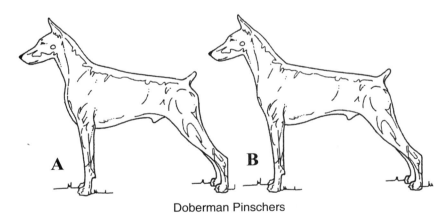

Doberman Pinschers

Doberman Pinscher A or B?

Structure, good and poor, has an impact on balance. One of these two Dobes has better structure than the other, hence better balance. The less well put together of the two is balanced, but only because he is equally poor in front and rear. In the show ring three of the virtues you look for in this breed are absent on the poorly structured example — what are they?

Both of these Dobes are the required square having the same length of body as height, but if Dog B possessed two of the three missing virtues his body would be long. Have you determined what the three absent virtues are?

The first missing virtue is a degree of forechest. The second is the shelf over the buttocks under the tail. The third is the absence of "pronounced withers" without which a hands-on examination of the shoulders would find a lack of required length and angulation, and the upper arm would be found to be steep and usually short. Therefore I would pick A over B in this example.

Brittany A or B?

Both of these Brittanys are balanced but each represents a form of "international" balance. Which dog do you prefer? If you were judging in Europe under the FCI you would probably put up Dog A. If you were judging in North American you would, based on the AKC Standard, probably place Dog B first. There is an American ideal Brittany balance and a European Brittany balance. If you judge internationally you must appreciate both.

Brittanys

Exaggerations

There are always exaggerated individuals within any breed and it is important to recognize excess for what it is and to act accordingly. Which one of these Kerry Blue Terriers is correctly balanced? In what way is the other Kerry unbalanced? This form of exaggeration—the second or lower thigh too long—is bred for in some

Kerry Blue Terriers

quarters, balance being in the eye of the beholder. This overly long second thigh has crept into a number of breeds including the Wire Fox Terrier, the Miniature Schnauzer, the American Cocker Spaniel and, lately, the Soft Coated Wheaten Terrier. Moved and viewed in profile, the extra-long second thigh is seen to cause the hind leg to over extend rearward wastefully high in a round, bicycle-like pedal action in order to maintain coordination with the much shorter front legs. Dog B shows the correct balance.

There are times when exaggerated balance is of value to the breed. The example that comes easiest to mind is Bull Terrier downface. It was in 1917 in England that a Bull Terrier was found to have an exaggerated profile (Head A). Fifty years later what was an indication of downface in 1917 had grown to a fabulous, egg shaped head (Head B).

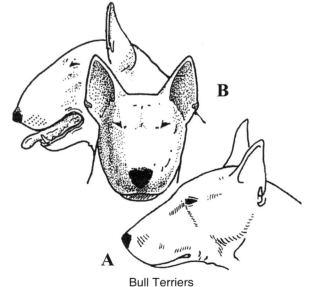

Bull Terriers

Much the same applies to breeds such as the Pekingese and the Bulldog whose balance is completely different from other breeds. In these breeds exaggerated balance must be bred for or type is lost.

Pekingese and Bulldog

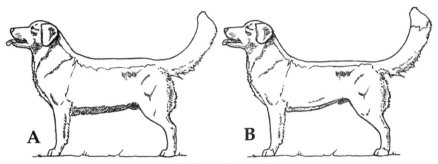

Nova Scotia Duck Tolling Retrievers

Know the Purpose

The difference in balance between these two Nova Scotia Duck Tolling Retrievers has nothing to do with basic soundness. Both of these dogs are sound. The differences have to do with the ability to excel doing the task it was designed for.

The Toller was developed some 150 years ago by duck hunters in Southwestern Nova Scotia to toll (or lure) wildfowl within gunshot range by duplicating that enticing action of the Eastern red fox. Similar to the red fox, the tolling dog runs, jumps, and plays along the shoreline in full view of ducks, occasionally disappearing from sight and then quickly reappearing, aided by the hidden hunter who throws sticks or a ball for the dog. The dog's playful actions arouse the curiosity of the ducks swimming offshore, and they are lured within gunshot range. The Toller is subsequently sent out to retrieve the dead or wounded birds, a job he does extremely well, thanks to this breed's great desire to retrieve and outstanding swimming ability.

Awareness of the Toller's task is sufficient to enable you to decide which dog is correctly balanced. Four departures from correct balance should be fairly obvious: The four departures are: 1) a thick neck; 2) too deep and heavy a front; 3) insufficient tuck-up; and 4) an overly long rear pastern. Dog B would be preferred.

Cairn Terrier A or B?

Which of these Cairn Terriers is more balanced? Does the Cairn you selected as balanced fulfill the Standard's requirement for body and legs to be of medium length? If your preference is for Dog B's balance you are not alone. Many people like Dog B's compactness. He is three-fourths of an inch shorter in body and

Cairn Terriers

has almost the same short leg as Dog A. The shorter body and legs produce a balance quite different from more typical Dog A. But balance is not enough. This is where Cairn type in terms of correct proportions becomes important. A good Cairn is compact but not too short in back, and with good length of leg so there is plenty of daylight to be seen beneath the dog. Dog A represents, in my opinion, the intent of the Standard.

Irish Setter A or B?

There is very little balance similarity between the Irish Setter and the Cairn Terrier but both need to have the correct balance for their breed to be good examples. One of these two Irish Setters is a good example, the other one draws attention to the effect of departures on balance. Which example is the good example and what features on the inferior example disrupt balance?

Irish Setters

Inferior Irish Setter A's muzzle is short and the finish to the muzzle lacks squareness. The topline appears concave and the forequarters too far forward on the body. In the rear the overly long second thigh further upsets balance. The example of correct Irish Setter balance Dog B has what the dictionary calls "harmony of parts," where one part flows smoothly into the next part, producing a pleasing whole. For instance, the muzzle is equal in length to the skull, the lines of the muzzle and skull are parallel, the muzzle (front) is squared off and the underline of the jaw is almost parallel with the top of the muzzle. It is important to overall balance that the head itself balances with the body. The neck is moderately long, flowing smoothly into nicely laid-back shoulders. The body is sufficiently long as to permit a straight and free stride. A long upper arm, angled back, sets the elbow rearward and level with the brisket, ensuring a degree of forechest. The topline as the Standard describes it is "from the withers to tail slopes slightly downward without sharp drop at the croup. This is a Best in Show winner—you must decide what is meant by "slopes slightly downward."There is a slight slope to the front pasterns and in the rear the hindquarters are not overdone.

The Impact of Grooming and Presentation – Two Examples

English Springer Spaniel

One way or another, balance is a trap into which it is easy for judges and breeders to fall. Like beauty, balance is in the eye of the beholder, and the beholder needs to know what to look for in each and every breed. These two American Springers are one and the same dog. The reasons for the difference in balance between the two are due to two things, grooming and presentation. Which dog's balance do you prefer? I prefer the balanced dog at right, however I am aware that many people are in favor of the more natural look.

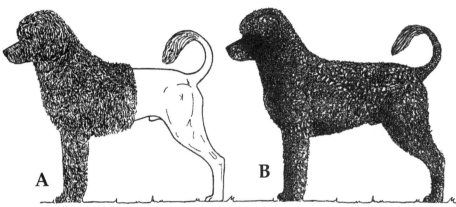

Portuguese Water Dog

Here is a Portuguese Water Dog with two different coats. Both appear slightly longer than tall but one is actually more than slightly longer. Did you notice that? An expert trimmer can take a Water Dog that is long-backed and minimize faults by shortening the coat in certain places and leaving it long in others.

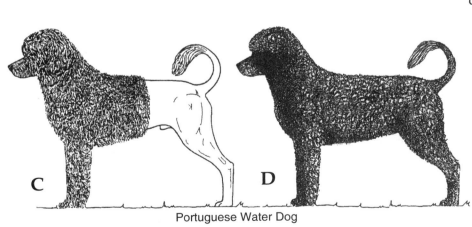

Portuguese Water Dog

In the case of a long-backed dog at left, the hair in front of the chest is shortened and the mane allowed to grow beyond the last rib. The effect will optically shorten the apparent length of the dog's body. An experienced judge will see or sense a departure from correct Water Dog balance and confirm his belief that the ribcage is overly long during the hands-on examination. When a Water Dog is short on leg, as with the middle dog, the hair on the brisket can be shortened to minimize the fault as with the dog at right. The reverse is done when the legs are overly long. Water Dog outlines are thus quite flexible, depending on the skill of the trimmer.

In Summary

The training of the eye to recognize correct balance is the better part of being able to properly judge dogs. But as you have seen, there is balance and there is balance. A dog poorly angulated both front and rear can be balanced and fool the inexperienced eye. Some breeds like the Brittany have a balance correct in Europe and another correct in North America. Some Standards do not provide details on balance, leaving judges to determine correct balance for a breed on their own. When this happens, awareness of breed purpose is especially helpful in formulating a picture of balance correct for a particular breed. Trends can influence this picture as can the quality of dogs the judge is exposed to or presented with.

It may well be that the ability to see balance is an innate gift. Most good judges have it and their hands-on examination of the dog merely confirms what he or she has already seen. However, the ability to see balance does not absolve the judge from constant study any more than if he or she had the gift of rhythm and desired to excel at many forms of dancing.

CHAPTER TEN
UNDERSTANDING SQUARE

Square is beautiful but because the norm is a rectangle in most breeds, building an understanding of square forces the fancier to take many factors into consideration. These factors include: forechest, height of withers, angle, and length of upper arm, length of foreleg, slope to front pastern, depth of brisket, position of elbow, length of back, length of loin, shelf behind tail (buttocks), amount of tuck-up and angulation front and rear. Square for a breed of dog is one where body length measured from point of forechest to point of buttocks is the same length as height measured from withers to ground. The Boxer, the Poodle, and the Afghan are among breeds that measure square from point of the forechest to the buttocks.

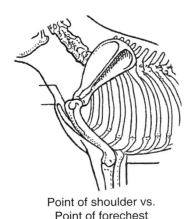

Point of shoulder vs.
Point of forechest

There are other breeds that are "approximately square." In these cases the Standards usually use point of shoulder rather than point of forechest to describe a dog that is approximately square because a degree of forechest isn't included. Interestingly, the square Belgian Sheepdog and the square Belgian Malinois are measured from the point of breastbone/forechest whereas the Belgian Tervuren is measured "square" from the point of shoulder — almost an inch rearward of the point of forechest.

These various physical factors combine in different ways to produce a variety of breed proportions within a square. Because of this variety, square breeds do not all move at trot in the same manner. It is important to understand the leg interference problems square breeds have at the trot and the manner in which each square breed adjusts to this locomotion disadvantage.

The Doberman

In addition to selecting the more typical between these two sound Doberman Pinschers, decide which one is more likely to excel at the endurance trot and which one is more likely to excel at the fast gallop based on four visible physical differences. These differences involve body length, tuck up, upper arm length, and angle, and

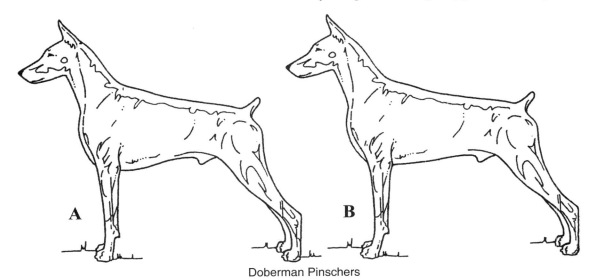

Doberman Pinschers

slope to front pastern. These four differences enable one of these Dobes to excel at the endurance trot but not the fast gallop. Since it is at the trot that breeds are judged, this would appear to be in its favor, however to excel at the trot this Dobe departs from type. Can you see in what way Dog B departs?

Dog A is the more typical of the two examples stacked in profile. He is square, having the same body length as height. His short body and flexible spine and good tuck up enables it to double up under its body to the same extent exhibited by the Basenji in the illustration below. All breeds are capable to this first period of suspension but not to this flexing extent.

Basenji at the gallop

Doberman B is the less typical of these two examples and could not gallop as fast as square Doberman A because (and this is where the four differences come in): 1) he is longer than tall; 2) he doesn't have sufficient tuck-up; 3) his longer upper arm positions the elbow further rearward on the body; 4) which in turn is complemented by a front pastern with greater slope bringing the center of support forward under a more angulated front.

Now, look at two more Dobes in profile at the trot in the show ring, the advantage is with the longer rather than square Dobe D. Having the same length of leg from elbow to foot as square Dobe C but with a longer body, Dobe D can incorporate greater angulation and trot with greater speed and ease. Square Dobe C is at a distinct disadvantage at the trot because space is at a

Doberman Pinschers at the trot

premium under his body. Synchronized leg action is more critical and if imbalanced, overangulated, or moved too fast he will be forced to over-reach and crab to avoid leg interference. Notice that directly beneath his navel the right front pastern flexes only 45 degrees whereas the right front pastern of longer Dobe D flexes to almost horizontal during this phase. This is the phase where, during the change-over from one pair of diagonal legs to the other, there is a brief airborne period.

During the summer of 1995, while waiting at the Salt Lake City airport for a flight home after an enjoyable judging assignment, I wrote down a remark made by fellow judge

Anthony D. DiNardo and received his permission to use it should the opportunity arise. Viewing Dobes C and D at the trot in profile now is the perfect opportunity. Paraphrased it reads like this, "No advantage is to be gained if through a fault (as in this case Dobe D's action at the trot) a departure is rewarded as a virtue." In other words, incorrect, longer than tall Dobe D moves better at the trot than square Dobe C, however it does so because it departs from typical Dobe proportions and action. To reward Dobe D for being the better mover at the trot would, as DiNardo warns, be rewarding a fault.

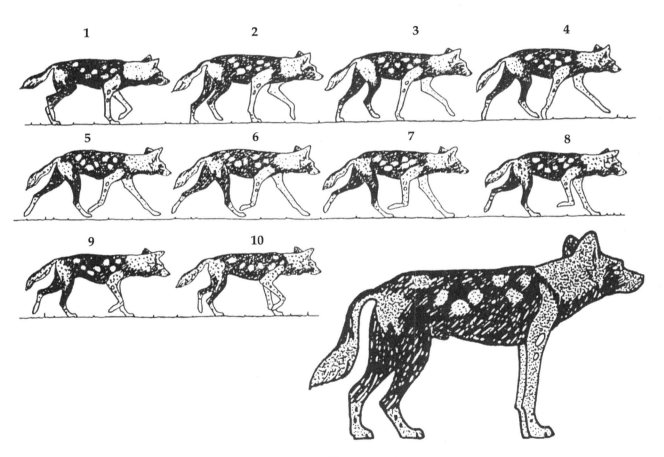

African Wild Dog locomotion

Understanding Rectangular

The trot is the gait used in the show ring to assess locomotion and the trotting norm is a dog slightly longer than tall. To appreciate the advantage of rectangular while at the trot, I have included an Illustrated Sequence of an African Wild Dog filmed at 54 frames per second.

Taken from my book *The Basenji Stacked and Moving*, this wild dog is doing everything right for a slightly longer than tall endurance trotter (i.e. diagonal feet relinquish support together in Phase 4; there is a brief period of suspension in Phases 5 and 6; and the opposite pair of diagonals strike the ground together in Phase 7.)

If there wasn't a period of suspension where all four feet were off the ground, and instead, in Phase 4, the diagonal feet continued supporting the body, then in Phase 5, instead of the hind foot slipping under the front foot, it would either interfere or over-reach. This is the point where foot synchronization becomes extremely critical for many square breeds.

The Tibetan Terrier

Square is considered so desirable by the writers of some Standards that they go to great lengths to find words that describe a slightly longer than tall breed as square. A classic example is the Tibetan Terrier.

Tibetan Terrier

This illustration shows an outline as seen through the double coat of a sound, slightly longer than tall, Tibetan Terrier. Parts of this longer than tall breed project outside front and rear of the square I have placed over her. The top of the square rests on her withers. This square conforms to the Standard's way of describing the Tibby as "square", (i.e., "the body length, measured from the point of shoulder to the root of tail, is equal to the height measured from the highest point of the withers to the ground.")

What the Tibetan Terrier Standard fails to mention is that there is a degree of forechest in front of the point of shoulder and even more degree of forechest in front of the point of shoulder, and even more (buttocks) rearward of the root of tail. The two combined add approximately 3 inches to body length. But Tibby fanciers declare this nit picking is beside the point. The point is that the writers of this Standard have managed to relate Tibetan Terrier proportions to square. My concern is that when the point of shoulder is used as a measuring point for body length, the existence of a forechest is often forgotten.

The Whippet

Revisions to the AKC Whippet Standard approved in 1989 and effective in 1990 left some degree of ambiguity about whether the breed should be viewed as square or slightly longer than square: "Length from forechest to buttocks equal to or slightly greater than height at the withers" — allowing for two ideals. With this in mind, which bitch do you prefer — the square Bitch A or the slightly longer than square Bitch B on the next page?

The difference between the square and the rectangle Whippet are obvious in the show ring. I remember shortly after the Standard was revised illustrating the two types

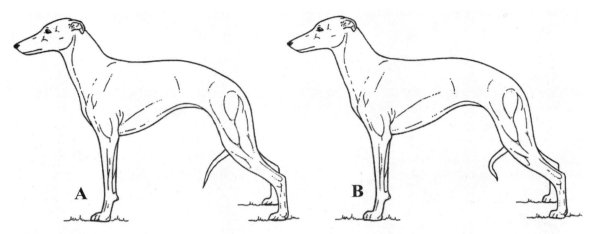

Whippet Bitches

and then judging a fairly large entry at a show where my best two Whippets were similar to those I have illustrated here. I went with Bitch B. Later I found out that both competitors had read my article and were very interested, since the two Whippets were otherwise of equal quality, if I would do in real life what I did on paper. I did.

You will find it interesting that in order to provide Bitch A with the same length of ribcage and vital organ protection as longer-bodied Bitch B, I had to shorten her loin. Shortening a Whippet's loin reduces flexibility at the fast gallop. The Standard advises "having length over the loin."

The Smooth Fox Terrier

Both of these sound Smooth Fox Terriers can be considered square. However, there is more to type in square breeds than having the same height and length of body. Dog A and Dog B are good examples. Which Fox Terrier is correctly proportioned within its square?

The Standard advises that the Smooth "must on no account be leggy, nor must he be too short in the leg." This is the hint. The Standard gives the height as 15 ½ inches and length of head as between 7 and 7 ¼ inches but shies away from giving length of foreleg in inches. The only difference between Dog A and B is length of foreleg. The amount of difference is the height of an arched toe. Dog A is the more typical of the two.

Notice that there is very little forechest. This is because of the correct short and vertical Fox Terrier upper arm and shortness and straightness of the front pastern—all in conjunction with a long, well-laid-back shoulder blade. This digging forequarter assembly produces action at the trot ideally suited to a short body.

The Smooth Fox Terrier's straight front ensures "the greatest length of stride that is compatible with the length of his body." Well said. Captured on movie film during the brief suspension phase, Dog C's legs

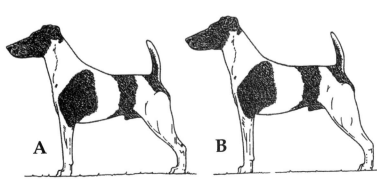

Two Smooth Fox Terriers

swing like the pendulum of a clock, the feet carried close to the ground, the wrist bending—flexing only slightly as the foot is carried forward under the body.

The possibility of leg interference under the short body is practically impossible, in fact during this phase and at show ring speed the chances are infinitely greater that there will be an unfilled space as in Dog D under the navel and little or no flex to the front pastern. Caused by a steep shoulder blade, the front leg lifts (goose steps) wastefully high. Seeing Dog D win does not make it correct. Did you notice that in the rear Dog D moves with sickle-like action? The left rear pastern does not fully open at the hock.

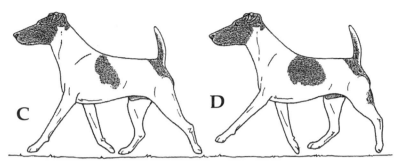

Smooth Fox Terriers at the trot

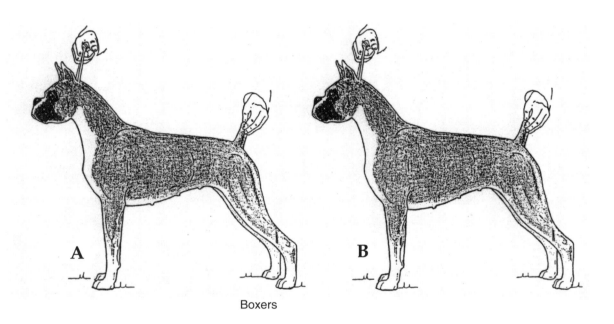

Boxers

The Boxer

Which is the better of these two sound, square Boxers? Both are the 23½-inch maximum height for bitches. Measured from the front of the forechest to the rear projection of the upper thigh each is equal to the height from top of withers to ground.

The better of the two bitches is Bitch A because the deepest part of her brisket is level with her elbow at half the height of withers, whereas Bitch B has more body depth than foreleg length. It is not enough that a Boxer be square, she or he should have a foreleg the same length as the body is deep, measured from withers to brisket.

Square is beautiful and has its advantages, but remember that square is not the norm. The norm for dogs is a body slightly longer than height at the withers, a rectangle. The norm is an endurance trotter. A square dog is not designed to be an outstanding trotter. A breed like the angulated Boxer is at a distinct locomotion disadvantage. Leg action, or better still, the timing action of the feet is critical because space under the square body at the trot is at a premium. When a square Boxer with correct moderate length of leg is not balanced front with rear he must make adjustments in order not to trip over his own feet. In doing so the end result can appear quite dramatic. In fact, wittingly or unwittingly, one particular action departure is preferred over correct action by some viewers captivated by dramatic but faulty action.

Captured on movie film at 54 frames per second, the square Boxers C and D are airborne during the change-over from one pair of diagonal legs to the opposite pair. (See below for a square Great Dane illustrated sequence for a fuller appreciation both before and after of this particular action phase.) One Boxer exhibits typical action and the other resorts to synthetic action. Which is which?

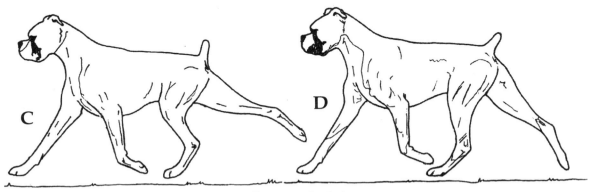

Boxers at the trot

Dog D's action is typical, all four legs reach forward and extend rearward an equal distance. You can readily see how critical the foot timing is of a square, well-angulated Boxer, the left front wrist flexing just sufficiently for the left hind foot to slip under it to occupy the spot just vacated by the left front foot.

Boxer at the trot — synthetic

This Boxer's dramatic action works even though it is synthetic. It is synthetic in that all four legs do not reach forward and extend rearward an equal distance, e.g., the right front leg reaches forward but the diagonal left hind leg does not. In fact, instead of slipping under the left front foot, it is well rearward of any possible foot interference. It works because this Boxer's second thigh is too long and over-extends wastefully high rearward. He has elected to employ a rotary hind leg action to extend the time not taken during the abbreviated reach forward of the left hind leg. Some Kerry Blue terriers and English Springer Spaniels employ this form of action adjustment. More recently, the Akita is guilty of this adjustment.

The Afghan Hound

Many square Afghans with a second thigh that is too long employ another form of action adjustment—just as this Afghan is doing. Instead of diagonal pairs of feet striking the ground together twice during a stride (two-time beat), each foot strikes the ground independently (four-time beat). If the viewer's attention is attracted only to the reach and extension of the two legs on the near side of the body and not to what is happening under the body, then this form of action adjustment can have great appeal. There is a school that is promoting the belief that this synthetic action is correct for the Afghan.

An Afghan Hound, in profile and at the trot

The Great Dane

I have drawn two Great Dane bitches – identical except for body length. Based on the 1990 AKC Great Dane Standard, which one is the more typical, Bitch A or Bitch B?

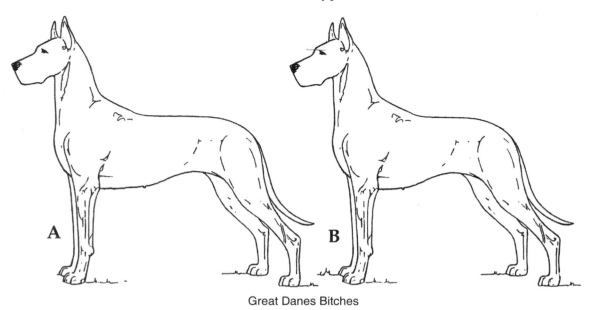

Great Danes Bitches

Unlike the Akita Standard, which specifies that bitches are longer than males, the Great Dane Standard describes the breed as square with the rider that, "In bitches, a somewhat longer body is permissible provided she is well proportioned to her height." If somewhat longer Bitch A is permissible, then square Bitch B must be desirable and therefore the more typical. Given that they are otherwise structurally identical, they will move in a similar fashion aside from one important action of which you should be aware.

This action pertains to the relationship of the two feet under the navel during the change-over of diagonal legs. It is more crucial for square Bitch B than longer bodied Bitch A shown on the previous page. When you trade off a square bitch for a bitch that happens to be "somewhat" longer in body (not in loin) but has other redeeming qualities you should be aware of the effect this added body length has on the following action under the body.

To explore this further, let's look at the Illustrated Sequence below.

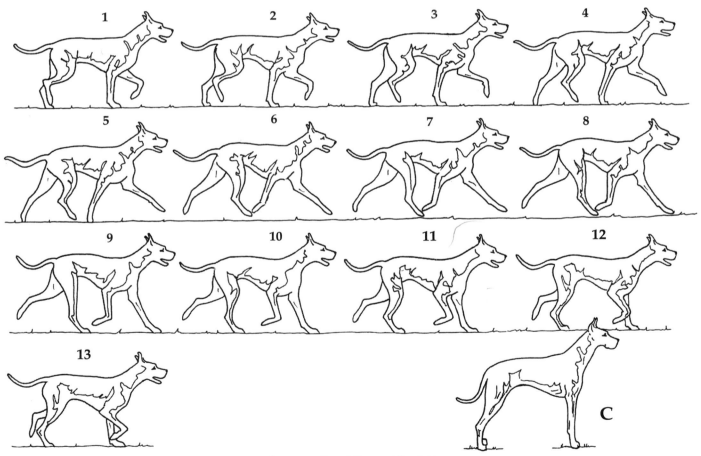

A square Great Dane at the trot

The square Bitch C's action at the trot provides an indication of how crucial the foot timing is for a sound, well-angulated, square Great Dane. This is close to ideal square action: diagonal legs relinquish support (almost but not quite) at the same time in Phase 5, and diagonal feet strike together in Phase 9. Isolated, her right hind foot slips under the flexed to 45 degrees right front pastern in Phase 7 shown here. The foot timing is critical.

By adding a couple of inches to the square bitch's length, Bitch D represents "somewhat lon-

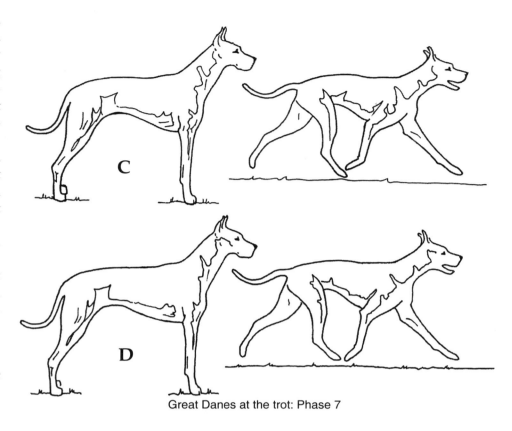

Great Danes at the trot: Phase 7

ger" stacked and moving. In Phase 7 there is no danger of leg interference because of the extra inches that were added to her body length. She moves in this manner because she departs from square that, you recall, is permissible in bitches.

Of the two, Bitch C is the most typical mover. Look at her again in Phase 7. If her legs were as free of interference under her body as Bitch D she would either be: a) moving too slowly; b) lacking angulation; or c) not balanced front with rear.

Note: Whether a square or a rectangle, the Great Dane's front pasterns should only slope slightly. Front pasterns that slope more than slightly when standing, and flex horizontal when trotting, depart from Dane type and typical action.

The Brittany

Which of these Brittany males shown in the next illustration is the best? All could be considered the required "approximately square," however their construction varies considerably.

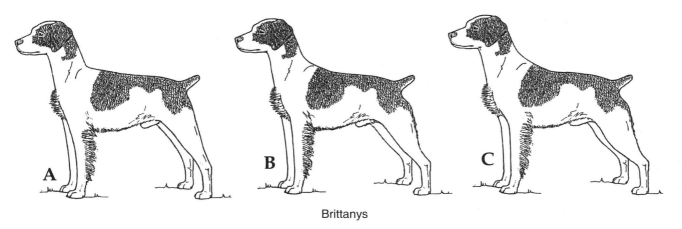

Brittanys

Dog A is steep in shoulder and upper arm, lacks forechest, withers, and buttocks (steep or short pelvis?), and lacks angulation at stifle and hock. He continues to have height and squareness because his steep shoulder blade and upper arm have forced his body to rise up above the elbow. Dog B possesses over-abundant power in his forequarters. He appears more square than he actually is because of the illusion of a shorter back created by higher withers. Dog C is the best of the three appearing so leggy that his height at the shoulders is the same as his length of body.

A Brittany action moving at the trot

Brittany action moving at the trot is another story — a controversial one. Question: Is it proper for a Brittany to over-reach at the trot in the show ring as shown above? The German Shepherd Standard is the only one I know that promotes over-reach at the trot, as long as the dog does not crab. I have included a German Shepherd illustrated sequence at the trot to ensure there is no confusion as to what over-reach actually is. For this German Shepherd it occurs just prior to and during the change-over of diagonal legs when all four feet are off the ground. A combination of specialized structure, great angulation, and speed produces this form of over-reach.

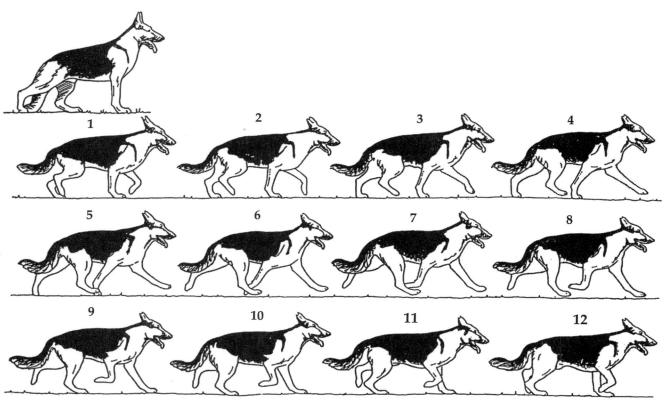

A German Shepherd at the trot

Under the subtitle Gait, the Brittany Standard advises, "When at a trot, the Brittany's hind foot should step into or beyond the print left by the front foot." One school of thought maintains that the foot cannot step into the print left by the front foot unless the foot, like that of the abbreviated four phases of this typical Basenji, reaches directly forward under and in line with the right front foot as it does with Brittany A.

The other school of thought maintains that the hind feet cannot step beyond the print left by the front feet unless the hind feet alternately pass on the inside and outside of the front feet. As of 2003, the specialists in the breed say "no over-reach" should be preferred.

A Basenji at the trot

PART II

FEATURES

CHAPTER ELEVEN
HIGHLIGHTING FEATURES

Many features need to be taken into account when a judge assesses a breed stacked in profile. The next two chapters will review some of these features with a large, short-coated Great Dane serving admirably to highlight those examined in this chapter.

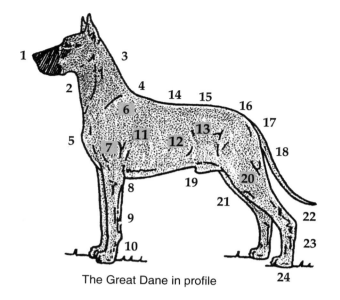

The Great Dane in profile

Examining the Great Dane

Here is what I look for when evaluating the Great Dane in profile:

1. Neck should be high set, long and muscular.
2. Neck underline firm and clean.
3. Neck well arched, gradually broader.
4. Neck flows smoothly into withers.
5. Forechest well developed without a pronounced sternum.
6. Shoulder blade sloping, forming, as near as possible, a right angle with an upper arm that appears to be the same length.
7. The elbow should be one-half the distance from the withers to the ground, the brisket extending to the elbow.
8. The forearm is strong and muscular.
9. The body measured from withers to brisket is equal in depth to the length of leg from elbow to ground; the elbow level with brisket.
10. The strong front pasterns should slope slightly.
11. The body is as long from point of forechest to point of buttocks as the Great Dane is tall at the withers—a square breed; in bitches a somewhat longer body is permissible.
12. Good spring of rib.
13. The loin is broad.
14. Back is short and level.
15. Top of loin is very slightly arched (not readily apparent).
16. Croup is broad and very slightly sloping.
17. The tail is set on high and smoothly into croup.
18. The tail should be broad at the base tapering uniformly down to the hock joint.
19. The body underline should be tightly muscled with a well defined tuck-up.
20. Hind leg strong and muscular.
21. Stifle well-angulated.

22.   Hock well let down.

23.   Rear pasterns appear to be perfectly straight.

24.   The feet should be round and compact with well arched toes neither toeing in nor out.

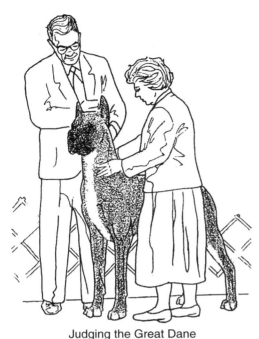

Judging the Great Dane

A Controversial Feature

As a means of introducing the features and the importance of each, I have selected a controversial feature for your initial consideration in the following illustration. This feature is correct on only one of these two dogs. What is this feature and on which dog is it correct?

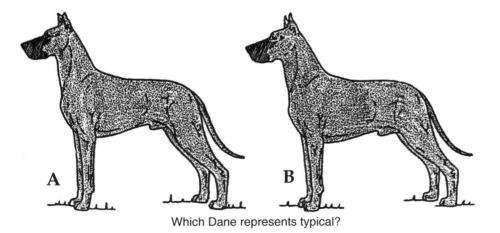

Which Dane represents typical?

The one feature difference between these two dogs is length of foreleg. In the 1980s there was a difference of opinion. Some people believed, as in the case of Dog A, the foreleg should be longer than the body is deep and the elbow level with brisket. Others believed that the foreleg should be the same length as the body is deep. The standard only required that the foreleg be straight. The March 1999 AKC Standard reads, "The elbow should be one-half the distance from the withers to the ground" and, "the brisket extends to the elbow." Dog B is the one that conforms.

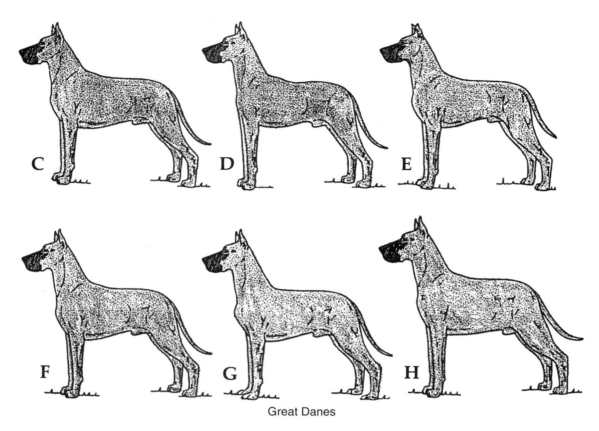

Great Danes

A Set of Examples

One of these six Great Danes represents typical, the other five serve to draw attention to the effect of two dozen physical departures on appearance. Once having determined which of the six best represents typical you are invited to identify the departures possessed by the other five.

Dog C departs in two ways: 1) the neck is short; 2) the body is long.

There is a great deal physically wrong with Dog D: 1) the neck lacks arch; 2) the neck doesn't flow smoothly into withers; 3) the body lacks depth and the elbow positions forward and below the brisket; 4) there is insufficient forechest; 5) angulation front and rear is lacking; 6) the front pasterns lack slight slope; and 7) the loin is long.

Dog E has three faults: 1) the forelegs are long; 2) the set-on of tail is too high. The third fault is not obvious—the front of the neck is not firm and clean.

In my view, the Great Dane in Dog F represents typical.

Dog G has three faults: 1) the sternum is pronounced; 2) withers are lacking; and 3) the toes are not well-arched.

The Dane depicted in Dog H is coarse, heavy and clumsy. On the credit side he stands more than 32 inches, (under 30 inches for males and under 28 inches for bitches disqualifies) but he fails to combine dignity, strength, power and elegance with great size. He is thick throughout, lacks tuck-up, and is long in rear pastern.

How Would You Place Them?

Based on the two dozen features presented as virtues and then as departures, place four of these six dogs in order of merit taking into consideration the seriousness and degree of each departure.

In my judgment, I would award Dog F as the closest representation of typical. I gave second to long on leg Dog E, not forgetting his high set-on of tail. My third place award was between Dog C, Dog G, and Dog H. The poor feet on Dog G disturbed me more than the pronounced forechest or low withers, although he did look more impressive with the short body, average substance and correct length of neck. Decisions, decisions. I went with Dog C. Down to Dog G and Dog H for fourth place, the latter's coarseness disturbed me but not as much as Dog G's poor feet, pigeon chest, and low withers.

Viewing these six examples and applying awareness of the two dozen features, I am reminded again that they apply equally to many breeds. Jean Lanning, a British expert has written, "My final advice to all Dane enthusiasts is to make a point of studying the best in other breeds. Do not be anxious to rush out of a show on your 'early removal' card; stay to see the Best In Show, and ask yourself, 'What is it about that dog which makes him a great animal?' Whether it be Chihuahua, Cocker Spaniel or Irish Wolfhound, they all have in common the same fundamental merits which have taken them to the top show award." These two dozen features are part of the fundamental merit requirements.

CHAPTER TWELVE
HIGHLIGHTING HIDDEN FEATURES

Having reviewed the Great Dane, let's turn now to a breed with a profuse coat and whose Standard is less than explicit in describing these important hidden features. Under his profuse coat, there are almost three dozen important features that are taken into account when a judge assesses a Lhasa Apso in profile. Only seven of these important features rearward of the head are described in the 1978 AKC Lhasa Apso breed Standard.

The Lhasa Apso

Lhasa Apso

Exposed in the see-through drawing shown below are the seven hidden features that the breed Standard mentions depicted and numbered 1 through 7. You are invited to identify them.

Let's begin with the seven features mentioned in the Standard:

1. A line drawn from point of buttocks to the point of shoulder indicates that the breed is longer in body than height at the withers.

2. The body is well ribbed up.

3. The loin is strong.

4. The tail should be carried well over the back in a screw.

5. The hind legs are well developed.

6. The forelegs are straight.

7. Feet should be round and cat-like.

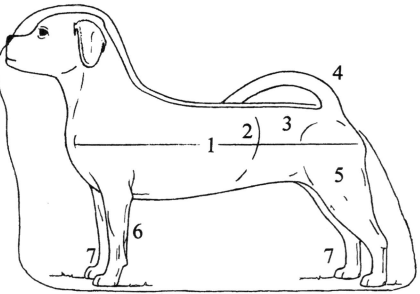

Lhasa Apso – hidden features

Exposed in the next see-through-coat drawing are 20 important features not mentioned in the 1978 AKC Standard — each highlighted with a question mark. You are invited to answer each question mark by identifying these 20 features assessed by a judge during the course of a hands-on examination.

Twenty Parts Not Mentioned

Question-marked in the illustration below, the Standard makes no mention of: 1)length of neck; 2) arch of neck; 3) height of withers (how much they rise above the topline); 4) amount of forechest in front of the point of shoulder; 5) length and angle of shoulder blade; 6) length and angle of upper arm; 7) levelness of back; 8) outline shape of croup; 9) set-on of tail; 10) carriage of tail; 11) length of tail; 12) shelf created by buttocks; 13) depth of body; 14) length of foreleg; 15) position of elbow in relation to brisket; 16) slope to front pastern; 17) height of rear pastern; 18) amount of tuck-up; 19) degree of angulation at stifle; and 20) degree of angulation at hock.

Lhasa Apso – 20 hidden features

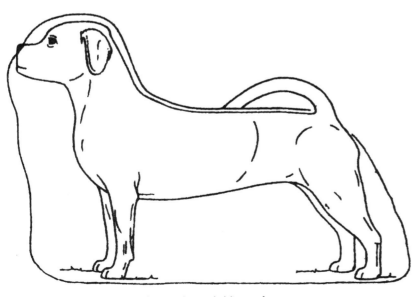

A see-through Lhasa Apso

Representing typical is the "see-through" Lhasa. The neck has sufficient length to carry the head well and is slightly arched; the withers are high enough to be obvious. The degree of forechest, although not pronounced, is apparent; the shoulder blade and upper arm appear to be about the same length and both are well-angulated. The back between the withers and last rib is level; the outline shape of the croup is fairly level; the tail sets on high and it slants forward, carried close to the topline and long enough that the tip can be draped to either side. The buttocks project beyond the tail to form a shelf. The body is deep and level with the elbow and there is tuck-up present. The foreleg is shorter than the body is deep, with a slight slope to the front pastern. I have included the degree of angulation at stifle and at hock.

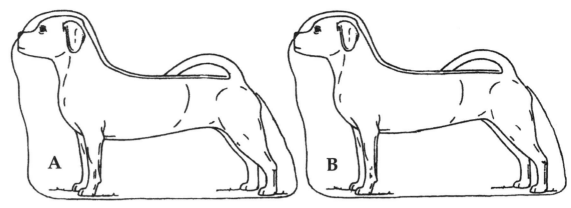

Lhasa Apsos

Hidden Departures

Not readily noticeable when cloaked — but obvious when not — the greater length of leg on Dog B departs from type in my opinion, especially when compared to Dog A. The departure is towards a foreleg the same length as depth of body (moderate length) rather than to my ideal of a length slightly less than depth of body (moderately short). Moderately short forelegs are graphically promoted (but not defined in the text) in Lhasa books by Francis Sefton, Juliete Cunliffe, Sally Ann Vsrvaeke-Helf, and Norman and Carolyn Herbel.

Lhasa Apso

Dog C is, in my opinion, a serious departure from type. The body drops down below the elbow in a fashion similar to the Shih Tzu, producing less height than if the elbows were correctly level with the bottom of chest. The hind end has followed suit, otherwise the front would be lower.

The Standard does not advise as to the ideal foreleg length or where the elbow should position on the body in relationship to the deepest part of brisket. Plus, being hidden under the cloak of long hair, if you did not know what to feel for, Bitch C could be considered correct.

Breeds with long, profuse coats require a hands-on examination. Standards unfortunately do not always describe the whole dog. In the case of the Lhasa Apso, in addition to the seven features the Standard does mention there are the 20 features the Standard neglects to mention, plus the distinctive head hidden under heavy head furnishings.

CHAPTER THIRTEEN
HEAD FEATURES

We are now going to focus on a variety of head features relating to expression and breed type while elaborating on the bones and muscles of the head. The examples I have selected are intended to provide an appreciation of the scope that is involved in a judge's assessment of heads.

Depending on breed, assessment takes into account the size and shape of the skull; the ratio of muzzle length to length of skull; width of skull and depth and breadth of muzzle; and if the skull and muzzle are on parallel planes. Then there is the texture of coat, the amount there should be, color, and color markings. Consideration of how high the ears should set-on is important as well as their size and shape. The size, shape, and color of the nose are checked making sure that the nostrils are open. The color and degree of pigment around eyes, lips and inside mouth may need checking followed by an appreciation of the strength of underjaw, the kind of bite, and number of teeth. Also, the size, shape, color and position of the eyes are important considerations.

R.H. Smythe in *Dog Structure and Movement* reminds us that there are four basic types of heads: the Brachycephalic (short) head as exemplified by the Pekingese; the Mesocephalic head as exemplified by the Bullmastiff; the Dolichocephalic (long) as exemplified by the Borzoi; and the fourth and most common head, the Monocephalic, which many dog breeds share with the wolf having a 3:2 skull-to-muzzle ratio. Dr. H.J. Hewson-Fruend in the March 1996 issue of the *Canine Journal* (Australia) counted 45 recognizable different heads going beyond the commonly recognized four head sizes, three muzzle-to-skull ratios, and five ear sets by pointing out that there are numerous other features which have to be taken into account.

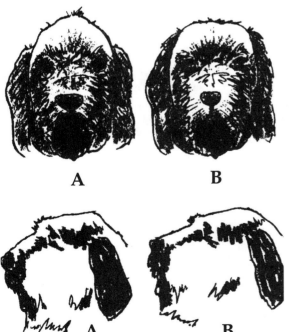

A   B

A   B

Spinone Italiano

Profile — The Spinone Italiano

The head of the Spinone Italiano is very unique. Viewed head-on you can see that Dog A has the desired oval skull with the sides sloping. The muzzle is square when viewed from the front. From the side, the muzzle is equal in length to the backskull. The planes of the backskull and muzzle are divergent (downfaced). The bridge of the the muzzle is, preferably, slightly Roman. Straight is not to be faulted. The muzzle and skull on the same plane or dishfaced are to be faulted and eliminated from further competiton.

The nose should be bulbous and spongy. Nostrils are large and well opened. Teeth are scissor or pincer. Lips fit tightly. The eyes have a soft expression, almost round, set well apart, lids tight. Loose lids are subject to debris in the field, have been a problem in the past and must be faulted.

Spinone Italiano A's muzzle is shorter than the skull and the stop is obvious. Dog B lacks stop and occipital protuberance. Dog A should be preferred.

Eyes—The German Shorthaired Pointer

Consider the effect on type and expression that size, shape and color has on the eyes. Two of these three German Shorthaired Pointers depart from correct eye shape and color. The GSP's eyes should be "of medium size, full of intelligence and expression, good humored and yet radiating energy, neither protruding nor sunken, almond-shaped, not circular. The preferred color is dark brown. Light yellow eyes are not desirable and are a fault. China or walleyes are to be disqualified." That leaves only one head.

In addition to their faulty eye size, shape, and color, the two faulty GSP's each have one more departure. Had you noticed these two departures from type? Aside from large protruding eyes, Dog A has a fault that on a Pointer would be a virtue. The German Shorthaired Pointer Standard reads, "Unlike the Pointer, the median line between the eyes at the forehead is not too deep and the occipital bone is not very conspicuous."As for Dog B, the GSP with the yellow eyes, the Standard reads, "The skull is reasonably broad, arched on the side and slightly round on the top." Not peaked as in this example. Dog C represents typical.

German Shorthaired Pointers

Head—The Bulldog

One of these three Bulldog heads is correct. Which one? What is the problem with the other two heads? The more typical Bulldog is the example on the far right—Dog C. He has the desired expression made possible by the correct positioning of the eyes. The Standard reads, "The corners of the eyes should be in a straight line at right angles with the stop (the stop being the indentation between the eyes)." The Pekingese Standard says it better, i.e., "The nose is positioned between the eyes so that a line drawn horizontally across the top of the nose intersects the center of the eyes." The eyes on the head of Dog A are too low while those on Dog B are set too high.

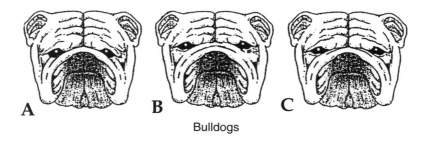

Bulldogs

Expression— The Japanese Chin

The Japanese Chin's expression is a breed characteristic. Viewed face-on one of these two heads exhibit this desirable characteristic called for in the Standard. What kind of expression should you be looking for? According to the Standard: "Expression –

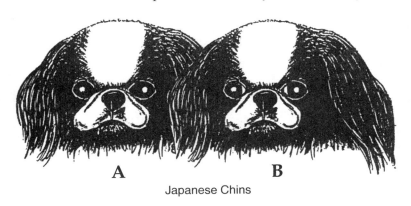

A   B

Japanese Chins

bright, inquisitive, alert, and intelligent. The distinctive Oriental expression is characterized by the large broad head, large wide-set eyes, short broad muzzle, ear feathering, and the evenly patterned facial markings. Eyes – set wide apart, large, round, dark in color, and lustrous. A small amount of white showing in the inner corners of the eyes is a breed characteristic that gives the dog a look of astonishment." Dog B would be the correct choice.

Muzzle—The Pointer

In Britain only one of these three pointer heads would be described as typical. In Canada the profile promoted is a different type than the British. Both the British and the Canadian heads are considered correct by Canadian breeders even though both

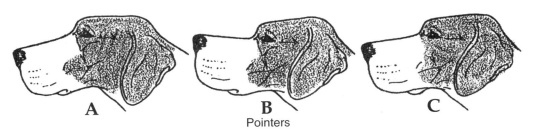

A   B   C

Pointers

are not promoted in the CKC Standard. American fanciers have a choice of either type.

The AKC Standard describes the muzzle as "Of good length, with the nasal bone so formed that the nose is slightly higher at the tip than the muzzle at the stop. Parallel planes of the skull and muzzle are equally acceptable." The diverging planes of Pointer A's skull and muzzle are incorrect for this breed while Pointer B would be favored over C.

Ears

A   B

Scottish Terriers

Ears are very important in some breed Standards and less so in others, however ears contribute to expression in all breeds. Some indicate a certain temperament. For instance for a Scottish Terrier to fail to show with head and tail up is to be penalized. The Standard goes so far as to say, "No judge should put to Winners or Best of Breed any Scottish Terrier not showing real Terrier character in the ring." Where the Scottie's ears must be erect as with Scotty A, the Whippet's must not. The Whippet Standard reads, "Erect ears should be severely penalized." Ear color can have a functional importance. The Bullmastiff Standard reads:"Ears darker in color than the body." Originally worked as a gamekeeper's night dog, dark ears, mask and eyes hid the head in the dark. The Collie Standard, concerned with the effect on appearance of prick ears reads, "Ears are carried about three-quarters erect, with about one fourth of the ear tipping or 'breaking' forward. A dog with prick ears or low ears cannot show true expression and is penalized accordingly."

The West Highland White Terrier's ear and eye placement is dependent on a broad skull. The West Highland White Terrier Club of America advises: "Regarding the head, the signature of any breed, please remember that the head engages the game first. As such it must be strong with powerful, punishing jaws. Such a dog is apt to have a broad foreface. With this broad foreface the dog will also show a powerful backskull wide enough to allow for correct ear and eye placement. We need you to help the breed by selecting for these features."

With this advice in mind if this were a class of four and your final decisions hinged on ear and eye shape, eye position and breadth of skull, in what order would you place them?

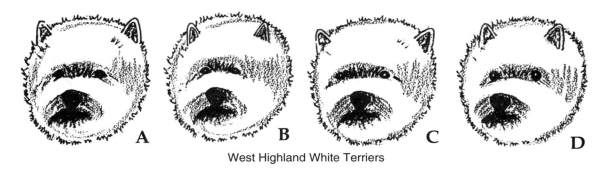

West Highland White Terriers

Finding the best ear and eye combination should not be difficult. Deciding on second and third best ear and eye features might take you a little longer, I am sure Head D is not one of the heads that you are considering for second or third. Even so, what is it you do not like about his ears and what shape should the eyes be? Answer: Head D has round rather than almond-shaped eyes and his ears are too close together. The closeness of the ears suggests, like Head B, that the skull is narrow. As for the eyes, Head B's are too close and Head C's are too wide apart. The choice of second place between the two is yours. Head A is my choice for first.

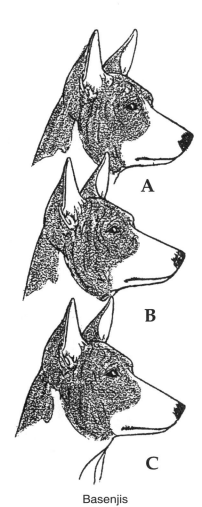

Basenjis

Muzzle — The Basenji

These three drawings demonstrate the subtle influence length of muzzle has on type. There is a growing concern among Basenji breeders with regard to length of muzzle. To address this concern I have drawn three Basenji heads identical in outline except for muzzle length. The white portion is the same for all three. Only one of these three heads has a correct muzzle length. Which one?

Basenji Standards worldwide call for a muzzle shorter than skull or a skull slightly longer than muzzle. Either way Dog A's muzzle is too short. Dog C's head is too long having a muzzle and skull of equal length. Technically, since the standard does not give a precise ratio, either A or B could be correct, but not really. In my illustrated book *The Basenji Stacked and Moving,* I depicted the correct ratio of muzzle to skull as being 5:7. I haven't changed my mind. I believe the middle head—Dog B—to be correct.

CHAPTER FOURTEEN
EIGHT FRONTS

Six Common Fronts

I have drawn six relatively common fronts that represent much of what you will encounter when examining dogs. The six bodies vary in width and depth. Can you suggest a breed to represent each one of these fronts even though they have not been drawn to scale?

I've given you a clue here: No. 3 is the Labrador Retriever which represents the canine norm.

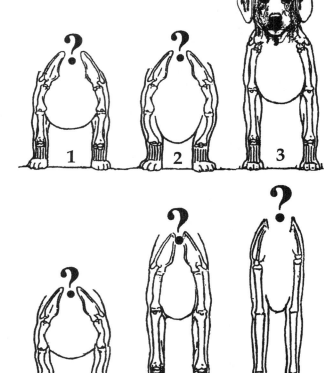

Six common fronts – which breeds are they?

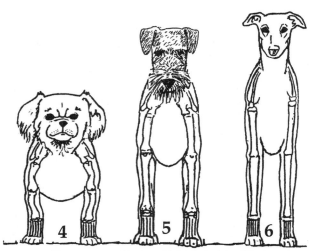

Six common fronts with breeds identified

The six suggested representatives I chose are: 1) West Highland White Terrier; 2) Standard Smooth Dachshund; 3) Labrador Retriever; 4) Tibetan Spaniel; 5) Airedale Terrier; and 6) Greyhound.

The shoulder blades on the Labrador Retriever serving as the canine norm are well laid-back, long and sloping, forming an angle with the upper arm of approximately 90 degrees. Shoulder blade and upper arm are about the same length. Viewed from the side, the elbows are directly under the withers. Front pasterns are short and slope slightly. The elbow is level with the brisket. The distance from ground to elbow is the same as the distance from elbow to withers. There is a degree of forechest in front of the point of shoulder. These highlighted front features that are part of the norm differ among breeds because each breed's conformation is based on the function it was designed to serve.

The West Highland White Terrier depicted here is a short-legged digger stacked in profile. The Standard calls for a well laid-back shoulder blade attached to an upper arm of moderate length. There is a degree of forechest. The forelegs are reasonably straight, the forefeet may turn out slightly. Length of leg and depth of body are equal.

The West Highland White Terrier

Next is the Dachshund with his specialized low-to-ground, wrap-around, digging front (the body drops down between the front legs). His wrists position closer together than his elbows. The front legs are straight only from the wrists down. The feet, as shown here, may turn out slightly. Viewed in profile, the Dachshund's forechest is quite pronounced. In skeletal form the shoulder blade is well laid-back and the upper arm slopes down and rearward. The elbow positions above the brisket. A form of the wrap-around digging front also works for the Skye Terrier, the Sealyham Terrier, and the Dandie Dinmont Terrier. The lower center of gravity wrap-around front also works for the Welsh Pembroke Corgi and the Welsh Cardigan Corgi, lowering their bodies so that backward kicks from cows pass harmlessly over their heads. The Basset and the Clumber Spaniel's similar low center of gravity brings their noses closer to the ground and reduces speed to that of a man hunting on foot.

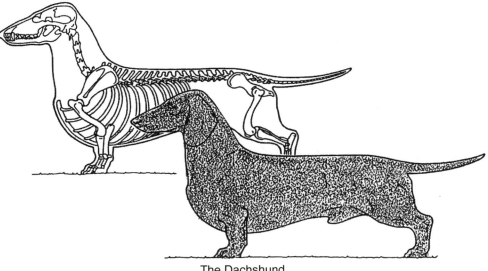

The Dachshund

The Tibetan Spaniel's shoulders are well placed, the forelegs slightly bowed, the elbows are level with brisket as shown here. Prized as a pet and a monastery watchdog, the bow in his legs were probably contributed by his common ancestors including the Japanese Chin and the Pekingese. The Tibetan Spaniel — although he may have a slight bow in his forearm — does not have a wrap-around front.

Tibetan Spaniel

The Airedale is the tallest of the terriers and it makes no functional sense that he have the same style of digging front as the smaller Fox Terrier. The sense is in the up-on-the-toes appearance this type of front provides. Stacked in profile the Airedale Terrier departs from the Labrador Retriever norm in a half dozen ways. Focusing solely on fronts, what are the Airedale's three major forequarter departures? The three major departures from the forequarter norm are: 1) the possession of an almost non-existing forechest; 2) the forward on the body position of the front legs; and 3) vertical or nearly vertical front pasterns.

Airedale Terrier and Fox Terrier

The other four differences in the Lab's front and the Airedale's Fox Terrier type front are more readily appreciated in skeletal form. Both breeds are seen to have well laid-back shoulders but there the sameness ends. The Airedale's digging front has a shorter, steeper upper arm and very little slope to the front pastern. This positions the elbow forward on the body and reduces the amount of forechest exposure. The resulting Airedale conformation provides this balanced, square breed with the prized up-on-the-toes appearance mentioned earlier. On the debit side this type of front reduces the amount of reach forward resulting in a somewhat straight-legged, showy action, the feet brought straight forward the same distance apart as the elbows. The Airedale, the Lakeland, the Irish, the Welsh, and the two Fox Terriers possess this type of forequarter digging front.

Airedale Terrier contrasted with the Labrador Retriever

The Greyhound demonstrates in profile the conformation man has selected for speed at the gallop. The shoulder blade is not as well laid-back as endurance trotting breeds and the upper arm is more open but not as open as the upper arm on the Airedale Terrier, and is much longer. The Greyhound's forearm is also proportionally longer.

Notice that the Greyhound's front pastern is long and slopes a little more than the Airedale and a little less than the Labrador. At the fast double-suspension gallop this pastern bends 180 degrees to lie flat on the ground, shortening the leg as the shoulder passes over it. After the Sighthound's shoulder passes over the paw, this pastern springs back up contributing an upward thrust.

Each of these forequarter styles has been selected by man to perform a specialized function resulting in a certain structure. When judging one of these eight forequarters one must relate it to the function it was selected to perform. A Labrador with an Airedale's short upper arm, or an Airedale with a Labrador's front departs from both function and type, both stacked and moving.

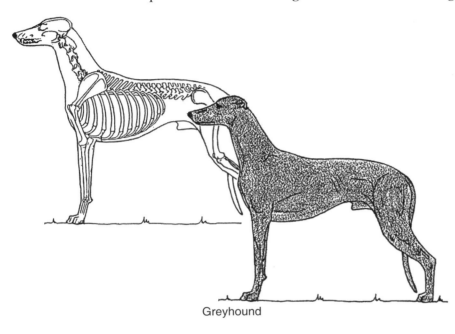

Greyhound

Two Unorthodox Fronts

The Bulldog gained notoriety for the so-called "sport" of bull baiting beginning in the middle ages. The object was to send trained dogs in to attack and overpower a bull. To do so the bulldog would, as the old-fashioned bulldog shown in this drawing has done, grasp the fleshy part of the bull's nose and attempt to "pin" him to the ground.

Bulldog

To rid himself of this painful treatment the bull would lift its head, dog and all, and slam the bulldog to the ground. To absorb the shock to the body this slamming produced, the bulldog was selectively bred to combine strong, straight, short, stout, muscular forelegs set well apart with a body well let down between the forelegs. If you can visualize the bottom of the chest striking the ground between the strong front legs you can appreciate why the elbows "should stand out well and loose from the body."

Once a functional front, this unique assembly is a major Bulldog breed characteristic. Awareness of the how and why each breed's front looks and functions or did function is an important aspect in the development of an eye for a dog.

The Bedlington Terrier also has an unorthodox front. Originally required to go to ground as an earth dog, the Bedlington Terrier gradually evolved into a very fast at the gallop, catcher of rabbits. His front is unorthodox in a number of ways, not least of all is the requirement for the feet to stand closer than the elbows. In researching the requirement for the feet to stand this close I was not able to find a reference relating to dogs. However in the 19th century a book by a Captain Haynes called *Points of the Horse* states that "It is common for fast trotters to stand with their hooves touching." I suspect this is why this stance was also promoted by the early Bedlington breeders.

Bedlington Terrier

CHAPTER FIFTEEN
THE FORGOTTEN FORECHEST

The Shetland Sheepdog

When I judge Shetland Sheepdogs, the first thing I feel for under the profuse coat is the forechest (prosternum). If it isn't there, there is every likelihood that the rest of the forequarters will not be correct and movement will be poor. Compare the absence of forechest on see-through Dog C to that of see-through Dog B to that of the same dog in full coat. The Sheltie's profuse coat can hide virtues and departures. Only a hands-on examination will provide the reason for imbalance or poor trotting action. Usually when the forechest is absent the shoulder blade and/or the upper arm is steep. British expert Anne Roslin-Williams in a *Dog World U.K.* article asks, "Has forechest gone out of fashion? This essential part of the normal dog, which lies in front of the point of shoulder seems to have been eradicated."

Shetland Sheepdogs

The Rhodesian Ridgeback

I have given these two Rhodesian Ridgeback bitches the same head so as not to detract from their structural differences. With their smooth coats, well muscled-bodies, and when positioned at the same angle, these two Group placers demonstrate a good forechest and a poor forechest.

Handicapped by a steep shoulder and upper arm, Bitch A's balance is disrupted by lack of forechest resulting in the whole forequarter assembly having moved forward on the body. At the trot Bitch A's action is restricted whereas that of Bitch B is not.

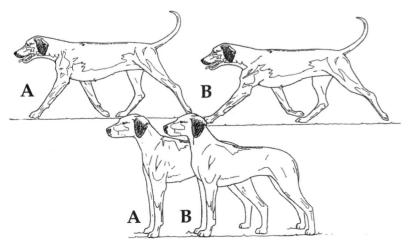

Rhodesian Ridgebacks in profile and at the trot

The Fox Terrier

Not all breeds are designed to have a noticeable forechest. The Fox Terrier (both Smooth and Wire Hair), the Airedale Terrier, the Lakeland Terrier, the Irish, and the Welsh Terrier all have an almost straight line running from underjaw down to the foot with only a small amount of forechest showing in front of the point of shoulder. Ideal Fox Terrier shoulders are well laid-back but their upper arms are intentionally short and steep. Fox Terrier action at the trot is a rapid pendulum with every little bend to front pastern.

Fox Terriers at profile and at the trot

The Weimaraner

In some breeds the desire for forechest can get out of control. While Weimaraner Bitch A could have better forequarters, she does possess enough forechest — whereas Weimaraner Bitch B has gone too far. The chest should be "well developed" but not to this extent. Unfortunately it's not always that simple. I know that Bitch B's forechest is too much of a good thing, however I am not enthused with either Bitch A's front, nor enthused with her long rear pasterns or steep front pasterns. So, despite the overdone forechest, I went with Bitch B. I guess a circumstance like this is an example that shows that an overdone forechest can be promoted in the show ring.

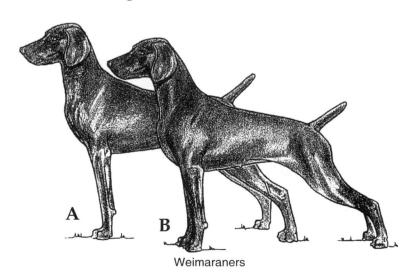

Weimaraners

The Tibetan Spaniel

The typical Tibetan Spaniel has an astounding degree of forechest. This envious degree of forechest seldom, if ever, receives mention. Why? Well, I have come to the conclusion that Tibetan Spaniel fanciers take this enviable forechest presence for granted. Interestingly, neither the Standard nor the American or Australian Illustrated Standard mention forechest, but then again they do not inform as to leg length or that the elbow positions level with the brisket. The only official information I can impart is, "The legs must be long enough to show a rectangle of daylight beneath the dog but should not have a leggy appearance." And, "the forelegs are slightly bowed." Does that help?

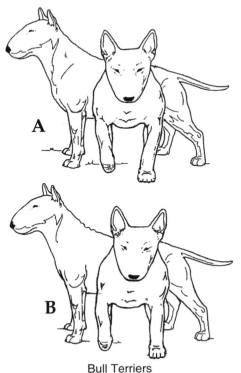
Tibetan Spaniel

The Bull Terrier

When broad-fronted breeds like the well-made heavyweight sub-type Bull Terrier (Dog A), moves coming, the foreleg is brought straight forward. The leg is straight from the elbow to wrist but not carried perpendicular—the feet tend to converge slightly towards a center line. When broad-fronted dogs are steep and short in the upper arm (as with Dog B), their forelegs are often brought forward the same distance apart at the feet as at the elbows when coming towards you. This wide action has appeal for the novice and the rocking action is sometimes mistaken for a jaunty roll. The loose rolls at the back of the neck over the withers suggest that the shoulder blades are not ideally laid-back.

A

B

Bull Terriers

The Puli

The Puli is not measured from the prosternum to the buttocks. He is thought of as "square appearing" so he is measured from point of shoulder to point of buttocks. The forechest doesn't receive mention but it should be there and it should be felt for since it is not easily visible.

Puli

The Tibetan Terrier

The Tibetan Terrier is mentioned three times in the AKC Standard as being "square or square appearing" when in actual fact he is rectangular. To describe the rectangular Tibetan Terrier as square, the authors of the Standard used the point of shoulder as a measuring point in front instead of forechest and in the rear they used the root of tail instead of the point of buttocks. In doing so they ignored everything in front of the point of shoulder and everything rearward of the root of the tail (highlighted here in black). The danger of promoting square in this fashion is that when the forechest and the point of buttocks fail to receive mention, over time these parts are often neglected.

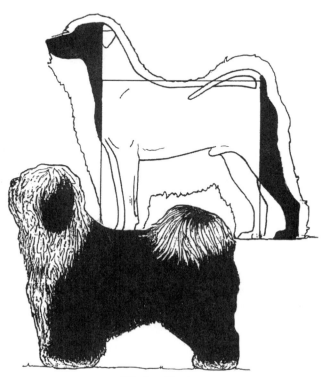

Tibetan Terrier

84

Ibizan Hound

The Ibizan Hound

The Ibizan Hound is described as simply "slightly longer than tall." The forechest or breastbone is sharply angled and prominent, however the Ibizan's brisket is approximately 2½ inches above the elbow and the deepest part of the brisket is rearward of the elbow. The Ibizan's front is entirely different from that of most Sighthounds, however in the field the Ibizan is as fast as the top hounds and without equal in agility, high jumping, and broad jumping ability.

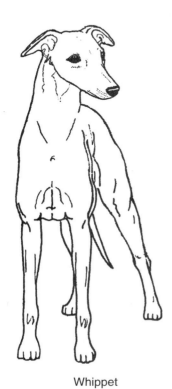

The Whippet

To ensure that the forequarters are correctly constructed the Whippet Standard warns of an exaggerated forechest and especially warns of lack of forechest. The wording of the latter is superior to that of any other breed Standard. It reads, "The space between the forelegs is filled in so that there is no appearance of a hollow between them."

Whippet

CHAPTER SIXTEEN
ARCHED TOPLINES

Toplines come in a variety of shapes and sizes, each designed to help perform a particular function. The norm is a topline level between the withers and the last rib with a slight arch over a fairly short loin. The Dalmatian below serves as a good example of the norm. The arch occurs over the unsupported-by-ribs portion of the topline called the loin. The strong, flexible loin contributes to the Dalmatian's endurance over distance at the trot and gallop. The Dalmatian's arch is very slight and I doubt if you can even see it in this drawing.

I prefer the term "topline" to "back" or "backline." The back proper is the vertebrae between the withers and the loin. The topline running from the neck to the tail includes:

1. The withers

2. The back

3. The loin

4. The croup

5. The sacrum

All five of these parts must be correct for the breed or balance isn't possible. Each of the half dozen breeds I selected for discussion here has a different balance as dictated by function.

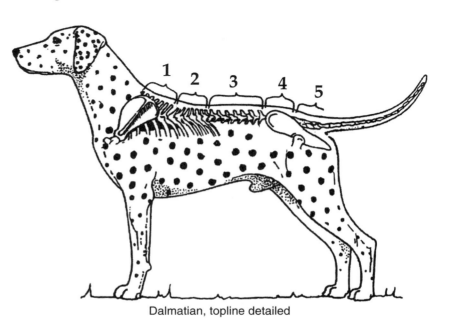

Dalmatian, topline detailed

The American Foxhound

The American Foxhound has been developed as a result of the type of hunting the breeder intended to do. He is used primarily for running in unorganized packs with each individual hound trying to outdo all the other hounds in the pack. The American Foxhound does his own thing, following his inbred instincts with very little control by man. In the process of this development the breed acquired a distinctive topline that is easier for me to depict than describe.

Based on the AKC breed Standard, which one of these two

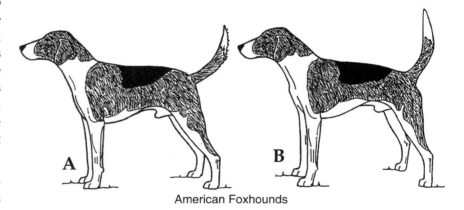

American Foxhounds

American Foxhounds best re-presents typical? Their toplines are different as is their balance. Would it help if I quoted from the Standard? The Standard reads: "Back moderately long, muscular and strong, loins broad and slightly arched" and, "Defects — Very long or swayed or roached back." That did not help much—the wording applies equally to both examples. Let me give you a hint. One of the two has an incorrect, heavy English Foxhound look about him.

The example that best represents typical is Dog B. This example conveys the essence of the American Foxhound, appearing speedy, well muscled with a slight arch over the loin and a tail set moderately high. The resulting distinctive topline contributes greatly to setting this breed apart.

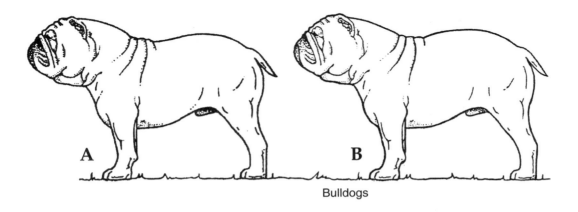

Bulldogs

The Bulldog

The Bulldog Standard asks for a roach back or "wheel back" topline. The complete description reads:

> There should be slight fall in the back, close behind the shoulders (its lowest part), whence the spine should rise to the loins (the top of which should be higher than the top of the shoulders), thence, curving again more suddenly to the tail, forming an arch (a very distinctive feature of the breed), termed "roach back" or, more correctly, "wheel back."

Here are two drawings of Bulldogs that fit that definition. One of these two is correct. It is no easy matter for breeders to get the Bulldog's topline just right and, with the variety of toplines presented, many judges also find it is no easy matter to determine what a desirable "roach back" is. Perhaps the word "roach" is not the best choice of words because it means different things to people outside of the Bulldog circle, however, "should rise to the loins" means the same to all. Which topline is correct for this breed? Dog A's arch is correctly over the loin, Dog B's camel-like longer arch is incorrectly over the back and loin.

The Dandie Dinmont Terrier

Originally bred to go to ground, the Dandie's topline is quite unique. The Standard describes it: "The topline is rather low at the shoulder, having a slight downward curve and a corresponding arch over the loins, with a very slight gradual drop from the top of the loins to the root of the tail." The outline is a continuous flow from the crest of the neck to the top of the tail.

Depending on how you interpret "rather," "slight" and "gradual" any one of these three Dandie Dinmont Terriers could have the correct topline but, in my opinion and that of knowledgeable breeders, only one is correct. In your opinion which one is it?

Dog C is out of the running — notice where his arch is. It is over his croup rather than over the unsupported (rearward of the ribcage) loin. That leaves Dog A and Dog B. If you chose Dog A you are not alone. I have used this outline in the past believing I had interpreted the wording correctly — however I hadn't. I made two errors. Going back to the Standard it asks for, "a corresponding arch over the loin." The highest point on Dog A's arch is too far rearward to be over the loin. The Standard also asks for, "a very slight, gradual drop from the top of the loin to the root of the tail." Dog A's croup drops off too quickly. The topline on Dog B shows the two errors corrected. The loin is now directly under the arch and the croup drop off is more gradual.

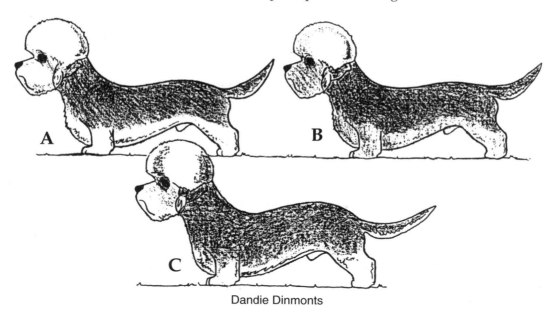

Dandie Dinmonts

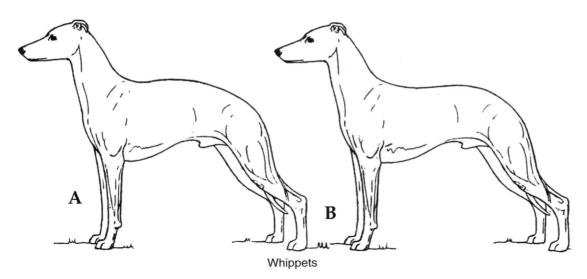

Whippets

The Whippet

The Whippet Standard calls the topline a backline and describes it as "runs smoothly from the withers with a graceful natural arch, not too accentuated, beginning over the loin and carrying through over the croup." The words "beginning over the loin" rules out one of these Whippets as does "over the croup." The toplines on each run smoothly down the neck, over the withers, the back, the loin and the croup but the arch in the topline differs in where it begins and reaches its highest point. The arch on Dog B correctly begins near the last rib and reaches its highest point above the loin. Dog A's arch begins closer to the withers and its high point is over the back.

There is a similarity in topline structure between the Whippet and the Bulldog. Both call for a marked arch over their loin but to serve quite different purposes. The Whippet's loin must be well arched to allow his hind legs to reach well forward to produce maximum propulsion and speed at the fast gallop, whereas the Bulldog's loin must also be arched to enable him to get his hindlegs well under his body but for a different reason, i.e., to give him the strongest possible purchase with his hind feet to pull back having attached himself to a part of the Bull.

It is interesting that the same shaped loin serves one breed to propel the dog forward at a fast rate of speed while the other's function is to prevent the body from moving forward.

The Old English Sheepdog

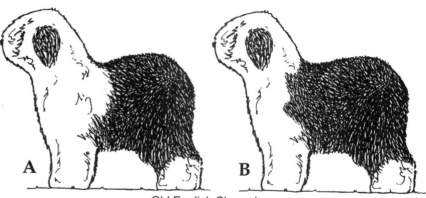

Old English Sheepdogs

Hidden under a profuse coat of good hard texture it is difficult to tell without a hands-on examination if these two Old English Sheepdogs have correct toplines. Are you aware of the form the correct topline takes? The AKC Old English Sheepdog Standard advises that this breed "stands lower at the withers than at the loin with no indication of softness or weakness." And, "loin is very stout and gently arched." Then, to ensure that we are aware of the importance given this hidden from view topline, the Standard reads, *"Attention is particularly called to this topline as it is a distinguishing characteristic of the breed."*

In lieu of a hands-on examination I have produced see-through exposures below of what your hands would have found under the profuse coats. The two toplines are the only physical difference, one arched, the other level — the arched loin on Dog A being correct. The question now is how heavily would you penalize the level topline?

The arch over the loin being a distinguishing characteristic serves a function complementing his wider hindquarters than forequarters. The wide, stout, and gentle arch over the loin allows the bob tail to get his feet quickly under his hind end and lift into an instant gallop uphill much like that of a rabbit; the widely spaced hind legs generating thrust then reaching past on the outside of the narrower forequarters. A square compact breed, the arch over the loin adds to the length of topline when the dog stretches out at the gallop. It is also believed by those in the breed that this arched type of topline is stronger than a level one.

With this capability in mind and the admonishment in italics in the Standard that reads, *"Attention is particularly called to this topline as it is a distinguishing characteristic of the breed."* I would think that a level topline should be heavily penalized.

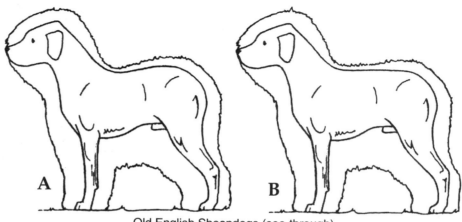

Old English Sheepdogs (see-through)

CHAPTER SEVENTEEN
THE SIGNIFICANCE OF LEG LENGTH

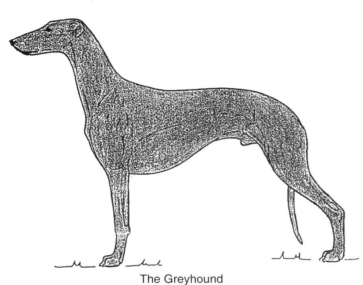

The Greyhound

What is wrong with this Greyhound's balance? In what way have I graphically modified this Greyhound to the extent that he could no longer excel at the fast double-suspension gallop?

Right, I removed an inch and a half from his leg length. Sighthound's forelegs measured from the brisket (the elbow level with the deepest part of the chest) to the ground are longer than the body is deep. This long leg length combines to produce superior speed at the fast gallop and contributes to a second period of suspension.

The Ibizan Hound

The Ibizan Hound is the exception with regard to level elbow placement. Such placement in Dog A makes its foreleg appear longer than it actually is. The Ibizan's elbow is positioned in front of the deepest part of the chest. Elbow placement, as you will see, contributes greatly to each breed's appearance. If you were to promote Dog B, an Ibizan with a brisket level with the elbow, you drastically change his appearance and, because of the longer foreleg, reduce his ability to excel at the fast, double suspension-gallop.

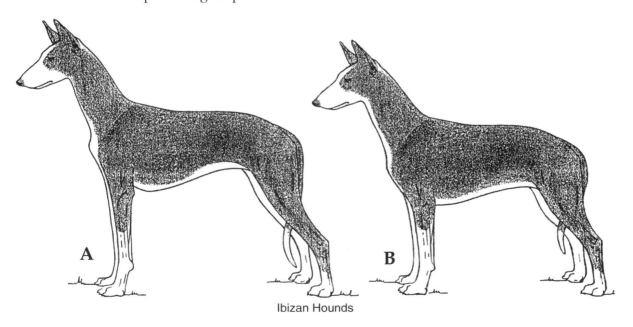

Ibizan Hounds

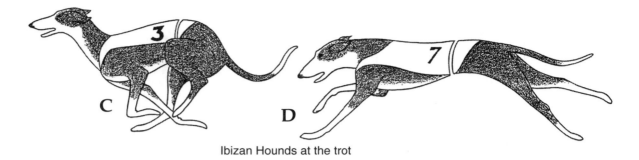

Ibizan Hounds at the trot

All dogs are capable of the first period of suspension where the legs fold under the body as seen with Dog C. Only very fast galloping dogs are capable of producing a second period of suspension where all four feet are free of contact with the ground such as with Dog D.

The Shetland Sheepdog

The norm for endurance trotting breeds is a foreleg equal in length to body depth, the elbow level with the brisket, the body slightly longer than tall. The Shetland Sheepdog is such a breed. Knowing the correct proportions for the Sheltie, decide which one of these two Shelties, Dog A or Dog B, have the correct proportions for the so-called norm?

Under certain circumstances, Dog B could appear long in body, however, he is short on leg. Breeders consider short legs a serious departure. Donna Roadhouse writes, "Height from ground to elbow, and from elbow to withers should be equal. Shelties who exhibit short legs are out of balance; one must remember dwarfism lurks in the breed."

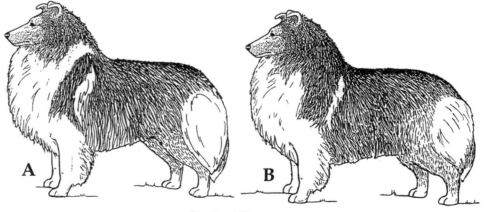

Shetland Sheepdogs

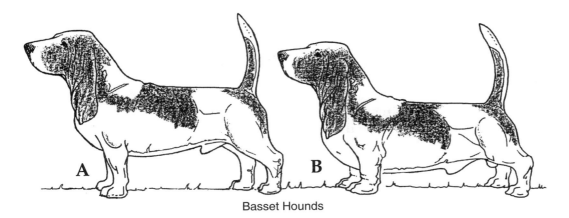

Basset Hounds

The Basset Hound

These two dogs are the same Basset Hound made different by elbow position. Some breeds may have begun with the elbow level with the brisket, the body eventually dropping down through selective breeding between the forelegs. The reasons for low-slung differ, some to slow down speed to that of a hunter on foot, some to make superior diggers, and for some, the lowering of the body was a means of avoiding kicks from cows. Basset Hound B is correct.

The Shih Tzu

The known location of the elbow is important in the judging of Toy breeds, such as the Shih Tzu. The profusely coated Shih Tzu has been one of the most difficult breeds for me to illustrate stacked in profile. The 1969 AKC Standard asked for a short, straight leg. The elbow on breeds with short, straight legs is usually level with brisket but this is not what I found when examining Shih Tzus on the table. I found many low-slung bodies, and forelegs far from straight. I needed to know where the elbow should position because its position greatly influenced structure and balance (oh yes, and height).

Shih Tzus

Let me illustrate what I mean using two sound but differently balanced Shih Tzus. Head-on and in profile Dog A and B differ only in position of the elbow and the resulting height. Dog A's elbow is level with the brisket, Dog B's elbow is positioned above brisket. Which Shih Tzu is correct?

When the revised AKC Standard was approved May 9, 1989, it included the sentence, "Depth of ribcage should extend to just below elbow. Distance from elbow to withers is a little greater than from elbow to ground." And, "Legs straight, well boned, muscular, set well apart with elbows close to body." This more comprehensive Shih Tzu Standard, in regard to foreleg length, provides a greater chance that, as in the case of the Greyhound and Great Dane, balance will be maintained. Dog A would be the choice.

The Siberian Husky

The Siberian Husky Standard foreleg requirement reads, "Length of leg from elbow to ground is slightly more than the distance from the elbow to the top of the withers." Requirement however is no guarantee. Too often the Sibe's legs are short. With shorter legs and given good angulation (better than longer legged Sibes) they look impressive running (fast trotting) around the ring without any danger of over-reach under the body. This shorter-legged, impressive at-the-trot variety have attractive heads and portend a new trend. Can the Standard's stated requirement for a slightly long leg foil this new trend? I doubt it. The significance of leg length as a draft dog is too often put aside in favor of show ring wins. This Siberian's proportions, especially leg length, have met with breeder approval.

Siberian Husky

PART III

MOVEMENT

CHAPTER EIGHTEEN
ASSESSING STRUCTURE AND SEEING MOVEMENT

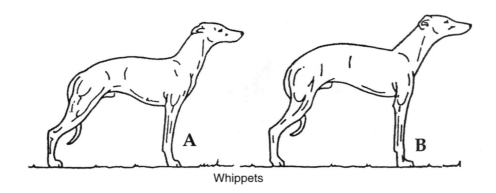

Whippets

In what eight visible ways is the better constructed of these two stacked, real-life Whippets superior?

The better constructed Whippet stacked has:

1. A smooth or more natural topline with the arch beginning over the loin and carried through the croup.

2. An arch to the nape of the neck.

3. A neck that widens gracefully into the top of well laid-back shoulder blades.

4. An upper arm placed so that the elbow falls directly below the withers.

5. A deep brisket reaching to point of elbow.

6. Sufficient forechest to reflect a fullness between the front legs.

7. A strong, flexible, slightly sloped front pastern.

8. A ribcage that extends well rearward.

Whippet B's structural faults serve to reinforce appreciation for Whippet A's structural virtues by placing the two side by side. Granted, the Whippet has a more pronounced tuck-up and arch over the loin than most breeds, however, much that is structurally wrong with Whippet B can also be applied to other breeds.

A Detailed Look

Beginning with the long, muscular neck it can be seen that the slight arch required by many breed Standards is absent on Whippet B. This is followed by an abrupt rather than smooth transition of the neck into the withers. Note that Whippet B's shoulder outline at the top of the blade is positioned more forward under the ear. Sometimes, but not in this case, this degree of shoulder blade steepness can cause the neck to appear short. On some breeds having not as tight a skin cover, wrinkles can be found at the juncture of neck and withers.

The faulty forward position of Whippet B's forequarters creates a hollow between the front legs. There should always be a small degree of forechest present. I consider the degree of forechest of Whippet A to be about right. I was pleased that the 1990 AKC revised Whippet Standard now includes the existence of a forechest.

The unsupported section of the spine between the last rib and the pelvis is too long on Whippet B and about right on Whippet A. This extra length of loin in combination with steep forequarters contributes to the accentuated unnaturalness of the wheelback arch. Usually when the pelvis is steep, the upper and lower thighs follow suit, but not in the case of Whippet B. The upper thigh and lower thigh are overly long compared to Whippet A, however there is good angulation at stifle and hock.

Comparing Action at the Trot

The best way to compare the action of these two real-life Whippets at the trot is in the form of Illustrated Sequences transferred frame-by-frame from movie film clips taken with a specialized slow-motion camera. It was not necessary for me to draw the complete cycle (20 phases) because the trot is a diagonal gait and the second half of the cycle is a mirror image of the first.

To enable phase-by-phase comparison the format I devised has each dog commencing the cycle with its right front leg in vertical support. The positions of the other three legs in Phase 1 vary from dog to dog depending on the dictates of their individual structure. This becomes increasingly more apparent as the sequence progresses and the positions of all four legs change dramatically between the two dogs.

To see dog locomotion at the trot in the show ring you should be aware of five basic requirements. The official AKC Glossary lists only the first three.

1. The normal trot is a diagonal gait, i.e., right hind with left front and left hind with right front.

2. The normal trot is a rhythmic two-beat gait, i.e., diagonal pairs strike the ground twice during each cycle.

3. Feet at diagonally opposite ends of the body strike the ground together.

4. Feet at diagonally opposite ends of the body also leave the ground together, i.e., relinquish support together.

5. And, most important but seldom mentioned, at the normal trot there is a brief period of suspension during the change-over of diagonal pairs of support.

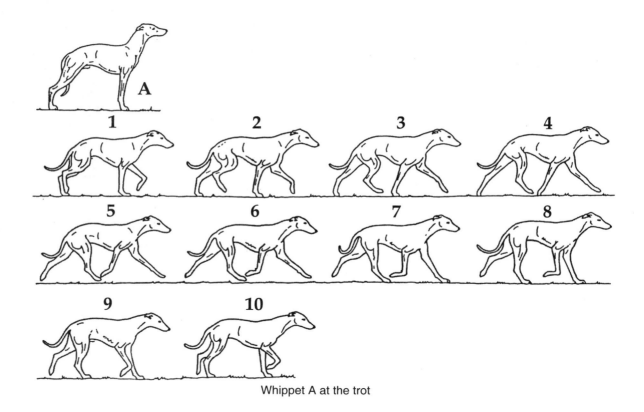

Whippet A at the trot

All five of these basic actions are accomplished by the better constructed Whippet A. Whippet B has difficulty accomplishing any of the four basic requirements and in addition departs from correct Whippet movement at the trot in three more ways.

1. In Phase 7 the feet of Whippet B strike the ground independently, one foot at a time, producing a four-beat gait over the complete cycle rather than the AKC required diagonal two-beat gait.

2. In Phase 5 the feet relinquish support independently rather than as diagonal pairs.

3. In Phase 6 the period of suspension has been reduced by poor structure to this single phase rather than the longer two-phase period produced by the correctly structured Whippet.

4. In Phase 4 and Phase 7 Whippet B is supported on one leg, a departure from correct action. At the true diagonal two-beat trot either two legs are in support or none.

5. In Phase 1, the left front paw is carried forward higher than the wrist height of the supporting right front leg.

6. In Phase 3, the dog hackneys.

7. In Phase 7, the right front pastern over-flexes. All three of these last faulty actions are employed by this dog to compensate for poor structure.

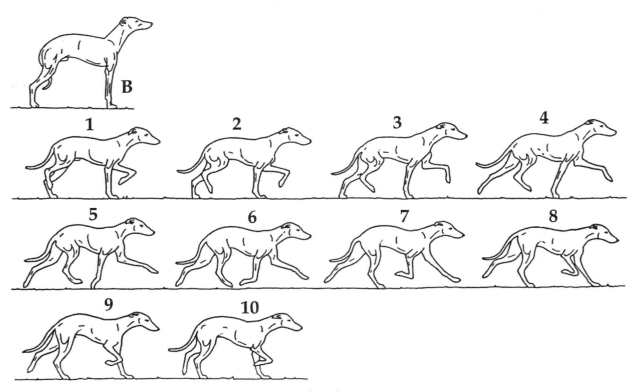

Whippet B at the trot

CHAPTER NINETEEN
THREE CANINE GALLOPS

What is wrong with the action drawing showing a horse at the gallop? If you know the answer you know more about the gallop of horses and some breeds of dogs than artists knew prior to 1877.

Edward Muybridge, using a line of primitive cameras tripped initially by horses' hooves, proved over 100 years ago that horses and many breeds of dogs are not capable of a period of suspension at the gallop where the front legs reach fully forward and the hind legs extend fully rearward. This series of eight outlines shown below traced from Muybridge's early instantaneous photography indicates that the only time all four feet of the horse are off the ground is when they are tucked under the body (Phases 4 and 5). As for reaching forward and extending rearward, the horse (Phases 1, 7, and 8) always has at least one hoof on the ground.

A horse at the gallop

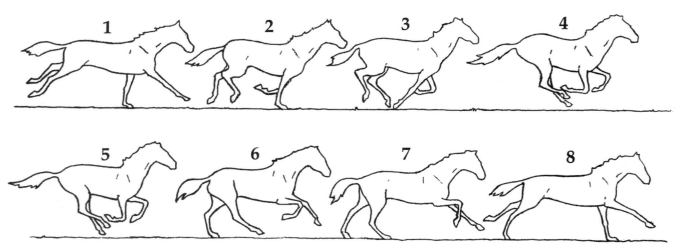

A detailed look at a horse at the gallop

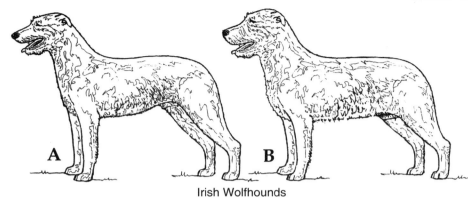

Irish Wolfhounds

The Double-Suspension Gallop

All breeds of dogs are capable of the one period of suspension where, in Phases 6 to 8 of Irish Wolfhound A, the legs fold up under the body. The degree of fold differs from dog to dog depending on speed and conformation. Some breeds of dogs, notably Sighthounds, are capable of a second period of suspension, one that resembles the impossible, fully reaching and extending positions for the horse in the first drawing. This second Sighthound period of suspension occurs at the fast gallop when the front legs reach full forward and the hind legs extend fully rearward shown below in Phases 16 to 18. To achieve this, a dog must be built just right, possessing hindquarters fitted for leaping, a very flexible back, powerful forequarters for thrusting upward, and a strong neck and brachycephalic muscles. Irish Wolfhound A is built just right, B is not. Can you see the nine reasons why?

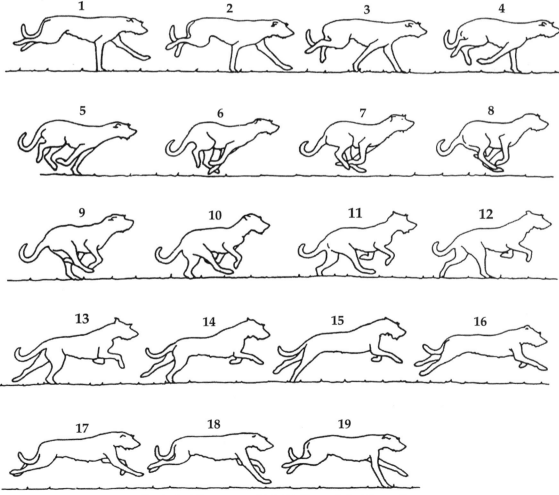

Illustrated Sequence: Irish Wolfhound A at the gallop

As shown in the previous illustrated sequence, Irish Wolfhound A is capable of a second period of suspension similar to what is physically impossible for a horse. The first period of suspension occurs in Phases 6, 7 and 8. The second period of suspension occurs in Phases 16, 17 and 18. Each of the four feet strikes the ground independently with a very brief overlap occurring in Phase 3 and Phase 12. Irish Wolfhound B would not be capable of this reaching and extending airborne period. Why? Compared to Dog A, Dog B departs from a typical Irish Wolfhound and resembles breeds that are capable only of the period of suspension where the legs fold under the body. His nine departures are:

1. A larger, heavier head.

2. A thicker neck.

3. A heavier body.

4. A level topline.

5. Increased shoulder layback.

6. A more angulated upper arm.

7. More slope to the front pastern.

8. Shorter legs.

9. Less tuck-up.

Phase 6

15 and 19

Irish Wolfhound B gallop detailed

Shown in detail here, the heavier Irish Wolfhound, Dog B achieves a period of suspension only during Phase 6, rather than in Phases 6, 7 and 8 as Dog A does. And, instead of airborne Phases 15, 16, 17, 18 and 19 he has combined 15 and 19 into one Phase where the right front foot strikes the ground before the right hind foot is lifted, similar to Phase 8 of the horse. The horse by the way uses the transverse gallop, the dog uses the rotary gallop.

The Half-Bound Gallop

The Brittany (next page) appears to exhibit the second period of the Sighthound double-suspension gallop, a mistake often made when photography at the gallop of a particular breed is limited to just this one phase. This Brittany's gallop is what I term half-bound. A good example of this form of gallop is exhibited by the Brittany working a field in the AKC Conformation Video. The half-bound is not generally associated with dogs at the gallop. Little has been documented on this gait in dogdom, none in my experience, and yet many breeds employ the half-bound. The main difference between this double-suspension gallop and the Sighthound double-suspension gallop is hind-end footfalls.

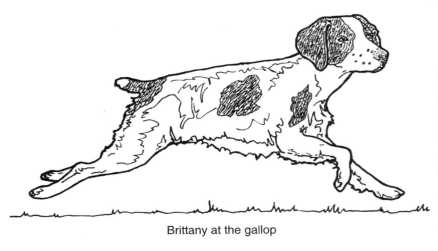

Brittany at the gallop

9   9

Compare the Irish Wolfhound in Phase 9 to the Brittany in Phase 9. Notice that the Wolfhound's hind feet strike one at a time whereas the Brittany's strike together as a pair. Now compare Phase 15. The Wolfhound's feet thrust one at a time, the Brittany thrusts with both hind feet at the same time. The Wolfhound has a four-time beat, each foot working individually. The Brittany has a three-time beat, the front feet working individually, the hind feet working as a pair, a less effective fast gallop.

15   15

Comparing the Brittany and the Irish Wolfhound

The Glide Gallop

The Dachshund and the short-legged variety of the Jack Russell Terrier (but not, to my experience, the Kennel Club's Parson Jack Russell Terrier) are, like the Dachshund shown below, capable of the double-suspension glide gallop. The foot fall is the four-beat, individual foot strike sequence of the Sighthound double-suspension gallop. However, due to the Dachshund's short legs, he appears to glide close to the ground.

Dachshund – the glide gallop

On film the Dachshunds that excelled at the glide gallop moved well at the trot in profile. Those that used the three-beat, half-bound gallop rather than the four-beat glide moved poorly in profile in that their hind legs (rear pasterns) never extended rearward beyond the vertical. Some that failed lacked angulation at both ends. Some with good angulation had too long a rear pastern (hock to foot).

CHAPTER TWENTY
THE TROT IN PROFILE

A number of years ago I was invited to write an illustrated series of articles on movement at the trot. Since dogs have been judged at the trot for over a century, I did not think I would have any difficulty finding published material on this subject. I was wrong. There was practically nothing written or illustrated on canine locomotion at the trot and what was available, in retrospect, turned out to be incomplete or incorrect. At the time I confined my drawings to a trace of a Group winner's photograph published in a national dog magazine, not realizing I was promoting poor rather than good action at the trot.

Artists traditionally rely on a single drawing to represent typical action for a breed of dog. Today I am of the opinion that the ideal is a complete stride—a cycle where each of the legs takes a single step. To accomplish this I have moved from single-lens reflex camera to a high-speed (54 frames per second) motion picture camera in order to capture the complete stride.

The Basenji

A sound, real-life Basenji represents a typical, good-moving example. The illustrated sequence in this chapter was traced frame by frame from slow-motion film taken with a specialized motion picture camera at 54 frames per second. The Basenji shown in the set of 20 drawings is taking one full stride—a complete foot fall cycle where each of the four legs takes one step. The sequence begins with the right front foreleg in vertical support, an innovative format that allows the action of individual dogs to be compared phase-by-phase to each other.

This example represents ideal trotting action as described in the glossary of *The Book of Dogs*, official publication of the Canadian Kennel Club and *The Complete Dog Book*, official publication of the American Kennel Club. Both glossaries describe the trot as "A rhythmic two-beat diagonal gait in which the feet at diagonally opposite ends of the body strike the ground together." There is more, much more, and using this example I will expand on the official description.

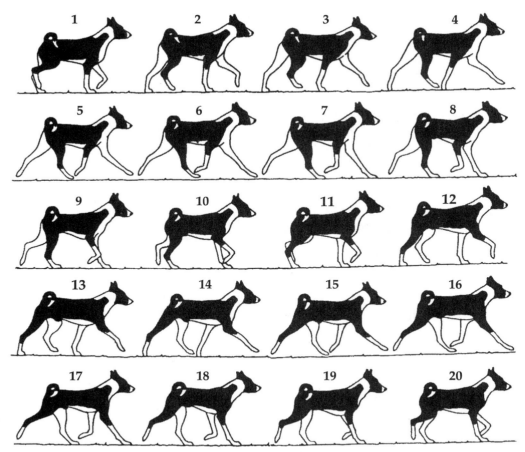

The Basenji at the trot

A Detailed Examination

In Phase 1, the front pastern is bent to support weight when the forearm is vertical. The rear pastern from hock to foot is also bent in Phase 1 and the right foot passing it is being brought forward close to the ground. The same can be said for the carriage of the diagonal left front foot.

In Phase 2, the right hind leg, still flexed, is carried straight forward close to the ground. The same is true of the front leg although carriage is slightly higher. Carriage front or rear should ideally never exceed the height of the wrist in the stacked position. Diagonal thrust from the two supporting legs is propelling the body forward.

Two-point diagonal support continues to generate thrust in Phase 3 and Phase 4. Unlike the lower head carriage of longer bodied breeds that excel in endurance trotting, the Basenji trots with head held high. In the past we were incorrect in believing that the hind legs generated thrust and the front legs only provided support. Now we know that the dog's front legs also generate thrust as well as provide support. Ideally, as in the case of this balanced example, front with hind diagonals combine to generate thrust.

As mentioned earlier, CKC and AKC official descriptions of the trot fail to mention that in addition to diagonal feet striking the ground at the same time, the feet must continue on through Phase 4 and then, as in Phase 5, diagonal feet must relinquish support at the same time. Only then can a dog be considered truly balanced front with rear.

In Phase 5 the left hind leg and the left front leg, each extending in opposite directions, can be seen to be reaching front and rear. This is equally true of the right hind leg with the right front leg.

For years official descriptions of the trot made no mention of this brief period of suspension in Phase 5 where all four feet are free of contact with the ground. It was first documented 50 years ago by the well-known student of canine locomotion the late McDowell Lyon, who in his classic work *The Dog in Action,* observed that normally constructed breeds evidence a brief period of suspension during change-over of diagonal supports.

Maximum reach and extension of all four legs can be seen in Phase 6. In the show ring it is the left hind and front legs that attract the eye. In actual fact these two legs are moving in opposite directions. It is the right hind with the left front and the left hind with the right front leg that move in the same direction. The period of suspension continues in Phase 6, the two airborne phases amounting to two-fifths of the time for each half cycle. Almost all the distance gained from generated thrust occurs during this brief period of suspension. To attain a two-fifth suspension ratio, diagonals must both relinquish support together as in Phase 5 and strike the ground together as in Phase 7.

The feet at diagonal ends of the body strike the ground at the same time in Phase 7. The front foot strikes approximately under the corner of the mouth when the head carriage is high. The hind strikes under the navel. The top line is most level in this phase but dips in the next phase as diagonals take over support. The supporting hind leg flexes slightly and the right front pastern in Phase 8 is carried forward at an angle, never parallel with the ground as in the case with endurance (longer than tall) breeds. Both hind and front legs are carried forward close to the ground.

In Phases 9 and 10, diagonal legs continue to support as the opposite pair are brought forward. For the full stride, Phase 11 would begin the second half of the stride as a mirror image of Phase 1.

The Dachshund

From the film footage I have taken of Dachshunds, I have selected one particular sound dog to serve as an example of typical movement at the trot in profile. The sound Standard Smooth Dachshund I have selected was a consistent winner, having appeal for both the specialist and the multi-breed judge.

As with the Basenji, this well constructed Dachshund is depicted in 20 drawings on the next page as taking one full stride, each of his four legs taking one step. This example's feet move exactly as required in the Kennel Club (U.K.) Glossary of Terms. The right hind with left front diagonals strike at the same time in Phase 7 and the opposite pair of diagonals strike at the same time Phase 17. Thus, this dog exhibits the desired two-beat gait, synchronized pairs of diagonals having contact with the ground twice during each stride.

In addition to diagonal pairs of feet striking the ground together there is also the unstated requirement for diagonal pairs of feet on opposite ends of the body to relinquish support at the same time (Phase 4 and Phase 14).

A second part of the phase readily seen but often overlooked is that the hock, as here, must open fully and the rear pastern between hock and foot extends rearward beyond the vertical. Usually when the hock does not open fully the front leg also lacks reach. The most common reason for closed hocks is too long a rear pastern (hocks too high).

Phase 7 is often described in official glossaries as "A rhythmic two-beat diagonal gait in which the feet at diagonal opposite ends of the body strike the ground together." This is exactly what this dog is doing. When Dachshunds depart from this rhythmic two-beat to a four-beat it is usually the diagonal hind foot that strikes first. The diagonal hind foot makes contact slightly in front of the pelvis and the front foot slightly in front of the shoulder. One of the more common departures from typical Dachshund movement is where, lacking angulation, reach is limited and the feet make rough contact under the pelvis and under the shoulder.

In the Phases 8-10 the diagonal legs actually take over support and the body is brought forward over these supports. The opposite pair of diagonals are carried forward close to the ground, the topline levels out. Support and the carriage of body over support continue through Phase 10.

In summary, a judge is better conditioned to "see" movement when he or she is aware that: diagonal pairs of feet strike the ground at the same time; feet relinquish support together as a pair; legs generating and providing propulsion both in front and rear as a coordinated pair of diagonals; that the front pastern is bent horizontal as it is carried forward; that there should be full extension rearward of the hind legs and reach forward of the front legs; and that carriage of head and levelness of topline complete the picture.

CHAPTER TWENTY-ONE
ASSESSING TROT DRAWINGS

Imagine you have been requested by a publisher of a proposed dog book to assess a number of drawings purported to represent good movement and arrive at a selection that will inform the reader what to look for in the show ring. The drawings are traced from action photographs which purport to show good movement at the trot in profile. The owners believe each photograph correctly demonstrates good movement. If they are mistaken, then they are making the same mistakes that writers and artists have been making in dogdom for almost 50 years.

Keep in mind that the current Canadian, American, British and Australian Official Glossaries of Canine Terms describe the trot only as: "Trot — a rhythmic two-beat (one beat each half cycle) diagonal gait in which the feet at diagonally opposite ends of the body strike the ground together (i.e., right hind with left front and left hind with right front.") That's it. One basic action. Actually, the official description describes the final action that the dog's feet assume at the trot, so that is where we will start.

Four-Dog Assessment 1

Let's examine a German Shorthaired Pointer, Golden Retriever, German Shepherd and Alaskan Malamute. Note that the feet of each have struck the ground in a different manner. Which of these four dogs can be said to depict the two-beat, final action correctly?

Before making that decision, realize that the movement at the trot in profile is more complex than viewing movement going away or coming and is at the same time more rewarding.

German Shorthaired Pointer, Golden Retriever, German Shepherd and Alaskan Malamute Assessment 1

In the show ring there are eight things a judge looks for in profile:

1. The degree of reach forward and the extension rearward of each leg.

2. If there is any leg interference under the body.

3. The degree the front pastern flexes and the rear pastern opens.

4. The height each foot lifts off the ground.

5. The carriage of the head.

6. The levelness of the topline.

7. The carriage of the tail.

8. Diagonal leg coordination.

The German Shorthair Pointer's owner advertised this dog's movement as good. At first glance, and if you were not aware that his diagonal right front foot and left hind foot should strike the ground together, this Pointer's faulty four-beat tempo might appear correct. However the striking of each foot independently suggests a front-to-rear imbalance. This has the detrimental effect of tipping the body forward. But there is an unusual benefit to this imbalance — the reach of the right front leg is prolonged. If only the reaching and extending legs on the far side of the dog catches your eye, as they must have the owner, this advertisement has great appeal.

This Golden Retriever — having correctly struck the ground with her diagonal right front and left rear foot at the same time — is a classic example of the final striking action. Her action conforms to the requirements of the official description. It is a two-beat diagonal gait in that during the second half of the cycle her opposite left front with the right hind diagonals will strike the ground together. Backed by official wording it is only natural that this final striking action is the one traditionally employed by artists to depict good movement in a single drawing.

Diagonal feet should not only strike together, they should also strike (the front foot for instance) forward of where the leg takes over vertical support. The foot reaches fully forward and then is retracted at the same speed the body is traveling. One must cancel out the other for the foot to strike without pounding; where the foot strikes is important. The ideal diagonal strike action photograph is, at the instant of impact, forward of vertical support. If the camera captures the action later than the instant of impact the supporting front leg suggests that this is where the front struck.

Pulling back on the lead has created the false impression that this German Shepherd's front reach and rear extension is greater than it actually is. This could be a Shepherd showing good movement, however the likelihood is that this dog has been trained to strain against the tight pull of the lead. This handler assistance is usually employed to improve a dog's front. The owner of this German Shepherd must have published this photograph without being aware that what he considered good reach and drive was made possible by two supporting legs that, prior to support, were moving in opposite directions. If this dog was not straining on the tight lead he might have been captured in the airborne period he should be in. We will never know. Notice that the whole left hind pastern rests on the ground.

Smaller, coated breeds that excel at this form of subterfuge are, for example, the steep shouldered Maltese, Lhasa Apso and Shih Tzu, their action partially hidden by long flowing hair. Of the three, Lhasa Apso and their handlers are best at this deception. Trained to pull against a tight (not just taut) lead held high, the race is on and the front feet may never touch the ground. With the body supported primarily on the hind legs the front legs reach dramatically forward, usually complimented by equally dramatic extension rearward (with minimum reach forward) of the hind legs.

Most exhibitors of these small-coated breeds have knowing hands that recognize steep shoulders, so they take it upon themselves to carry the front end. Given sufficient upper arm length, forearm length, and coat length, smaller coated breeds can be made to almost float around the show ring.

There is a correct degree of front pastern flex for every breed, from the full flex of endurance trotters to the minimum flex of certain digging terriers (e.g. the Lakeland Terrier). Degree of flex relates directly to forequarter structure. The most visible clue as to the degree a front pastern will flex at the trot is the degree the front pastern slopes when stacked.

The Alaskan Malamute's feet incorrectly strike the ground one at a time rather than as diagonal pairs, and he does something else that should disturb but often doesn't. This particular Mal's right front pastern is doing something unusual. His bent front pastern as it is carried forward over-flexes. Depending on breed conformation the degree of front pastern flex varies. The Mal's front pastern should flex no more than 90 degrees (horizontal).

Over-flexed front pasterns are common in St. Bernards and German Shepherds (probably because of weak tendons) but seldom in Mals. It may be a weak pastern or this Mal may be over-flexing at the wrist to extend the time the front leg is off the ground. The one hind leg support suggests the front is inferior.

It is difficult to determine the cause of over-flex from a single photograph. I believe that faulty over-flex is a concern worthy of addressing. In my all-breed, audio-visual, structure-locomotion seminar presentation, I freeze slow-motion movie film (transferred to video) and discuss each over-flex example frame by frame.

Four-Dog Assessment 2

As discussed in the previous chapter, the period of suspension in dog loco-motion has been greatly misunderstood. Let's look at this is in the next set of four drawings.

The trace from a photograph truthfully advertising a Schnauzer's good movement demonstrates one method artists use to get around this question — we simply leave out one important piece of

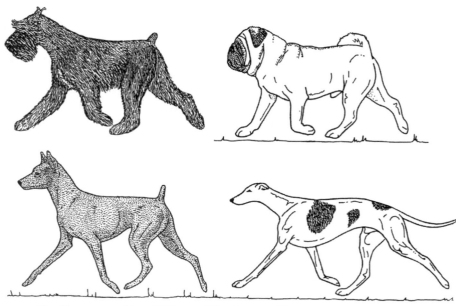

The Schnauzer, Pug, Miniature Pinscher, and Greyhound Assessment 2

information! When artists produce an action drawing like this one of a Standard Schnauzer they often leave out any reference to the ground. By not including any reference to the ground they avoid having to commit themselves to graphically answering yes or no to the question of suspension while at the same time providing more reach and extension.

Misunderstanding over-suspension is the main reason why many people have difficulty understanding and "seeing" action in the show ring. This misunderstanding is based on the mistaken belief that a brief period of suspension only occurs when the dog is specifically bred for it. If we are to believe the advice that for a period of suspension to occur at the trot a dog must have a long reach and move at a fast gait, then the likelihood of this sound Pug achieving airborne status should be zero. However, here he is correctly advertised as a good mover, all four feet are off the ground.

The Miniature Pinscher is certainly not known for his long reach or fast gait but here one is correctly exhibiting a brief period of suspension at the trot. He also hackneys but does so before diagonal feet relinquish support. The greatest degree of Min Pin hackney action or hackney-like action occurs front and rear when the Min Pin's supporting diagonal legs are perpendicular (forearm and rear pastern).

All well-balanced dogs produce a brief period of suspension during the change-over of diagonal pairs of supports. Notice that this balanced Greyhound, with all four feet free of contact with the ground, flexes its right front pastern (wrist) thereby enabling his right hind foot to slip underneath and strike on or beyond the imprint left by the right front foot. This can only happen because there is a brief period of suspension during the change-over of diagonal supports. Brief suspension is a necessity. If there was no brief airborne period and this dog's lateral right front leg continued supporting the body, the right hind foot would strike the supporting right front leg.

Another reason for the brief period of suspension is swing time; the time it takes for a dog's foot to lift off the ground, flex at the wrist, be carried forward and reach out, and be drawn back before it strikes the ground. At the walk there is a long support period and the dog has lots of time to lift and carry each leg forward. At the faster, normal trot however, the duration of support time is reduced. To provide sufficient time for the leg to be brought forward, the length of swing time must be increased to make up for reduced support time. The balanced dog at the diagonal trot does this by propelling its body up and forward into a brief period of suspension. This brief airborne period provides the time needed for the leg to be carried forward. It is during this brief period of suspension where the body is projected forward in the line of travel, free of slowing contact with the ground, that most distance is covered. Without a period of suspension, forward progression would be limited to earth-bound carriage of the body over diagonal supporting legs.

The Whippet, the English Setter, the Welsh Corgi, and the German Shepherd Assessment 3

Four-Dog Assessment 3

The brief period of suspension exhibited by this Whippet does not guarantee that its movement is good, it only indicates that this Whippet is balanced, all four legs reaching an equal distance forward and back. Notice the open space under her body. For this space to be empty she is either too long in body, has insufficient angulation front or rear, or she was moving too slowly when the photograph was taken. This photograph serves to remind that reach under the body should be taken into account when selecting a photograph.

The trace of the English Setter, where the right hind foot is slipping underneath its lateral front foot, is from a published photograph that mistakenly advised the reader that this dog's foot timing was excellent. Wrong. At this slip-under phase all four feet should be off the ground. This English Setter's strange pair of (lateral) supports was surely captured as the dog was coming to a halt. Having viewed thousands of feet of slow-motion movie film this is the answer I have arrived at. In addition, note that the right front pastern has over-flexed, which often happens as a dog is pulled to a stop or in making a complete turn at the end of the mat.

Breeds with short legs, even those with a long body and a wrap-around front like this sound Pembroke Welsh Corgi, exhibit a brief period of suspension at the trot in the show ring. They also open the hock and extend the hind leg fully rearward beyond the vertical. I take this opportunity to apologize for the non-extension of the hind leg of the Welsh Pembroke that I drew on page 149 of Curtis Brown's informative book *Dog Locomotion and Gait Analysis*.

This longer-than-tall, far-reaching, fast-moving German Shepherd is over-reaching. This suspended action is correct as per the wording in the Canadian and the American Standards (not stated in the British or the FCI Standard). Over-reach is not correct if the German Shepherd crabs—when the body deviates from the straight line of travel. This example's left hind foot during suspension is passing inside the left front foot.

The reverse will occur during the second half of the cycle. The result is a far reaching, elastic, seemingly without effort, smooth rhythmic gait. The fuller the diagonal co-ordination of his legs, the longer will be his period of suspension. In North America this fast over-reach action is called the Flying Trot.

A Three-Dog Assessment

All breeds can deliver a brief period of suspension without over-reach at the diagonal trot just as this Kuvasz does. This period of suspension:

1. Allows the hind foot to step under the lateral front foot during the change-over of diagonal supports;

2. Produces the maximum ground covered during the period when all four feet are free of contact with the ground; and

3. Provides the needed time for the airborne distance to be made, however no Breed Standard (including that of the German Shepherd) incorporates this fact in its description of gait.

Length of body and length of leg as well as angulation greatly influence reach. This sound, well-balanced Welsh Springer Spaniel has a moderate length of body, slightly longer than height and a leg of moderate length. His smooth action was captured with all four feet free of contact with the ground. He could serve to represent the endurance trot.

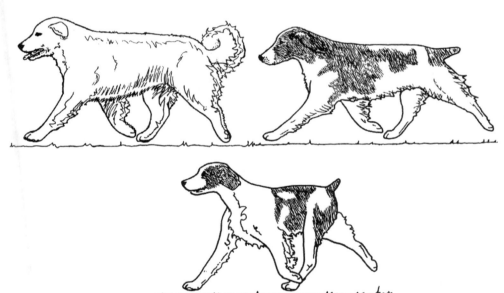

The Kuvasz, the Welsh Springer Spaniel, the Brittany

This square Brittany, (the body the same length as height), has a longer leg and over-reaches. He over-reaches because either he is over angulated or because he was moved too fast. Some judges have become conditioned to the square Brittany Standard and allow, even promote, over-reach. This is not the case in Britain or Brittany. The Canadian Standard (1994) and the American (1990) Brittany Standard advise that: "When at the trot, the Brittany's hind foot should step into or beyond the print left by the front foot." This direction is mistakenly interpreted by some people, perhaps a large number, to mean that it is okay for the Brittany to over-reach at the trot.

It isn't. The balanced Brittany, with moderate angulation moved at a normal show ring speed, steps beyond the print of the front foot without having to over-reach because during the brief airborne period the body is projected well forward of the print left by the front foot. This opinion is shared by people responsible for Brittany education in both Canada and in United States. Whether this shared opinion will influence advertisers to select less dramatic action or exhibitors to slow down, or judges to ask for the Brittany to be slowed down is debatable.

Dogs over-reach in the show ring when they:

1. Are moved too fast.

2. Are too short in body.

3. Are too long in leg.

4. Have one end stronger than the other.

5. Are over-angulated.

The German Shepherd is the only breed allowed to over-reach (without crabbing). In regard to the German Shepherd, I can only speak for Canadian and American German Shepherd and their respective Standards, both promote over-reach. The British Standard only asks for the hind leg to reach to midpoint of body; the FCI only asks for the hind leg to be thrust well forward under body.

A Five-Dog Assessment

In addition to diagonal feet striking the ground at the same time, diagonal feet should also lift together. Dogs captured with a freeze-action camera in the act of relinquishing diagonal support can provide an impressive photograph for advertising a dog's good movement.

There is no official rule that states diagonal feet must lift together only that "the trot is a rhythmic two-beat (twice in each cycle) diagonal gait in which feet at diagonally

opposite ends of the body strike the ground together." It would stand to reason however that a trot cannot be truly rhythmic if diagonal feet lift in four-beat time and strike in two-beat time.

Three of the five dogs were captured by cameras relinquishing support correctly — but only one is a good mover. Which one?

This Borzoi is correctly relinquishing diagonal support. The topline is firm and all four legs reach forward and extend rearward an equal distance.

If this Dalmatian's dramatic reach forward of his left front leg and equally dramatic extension rearward of his left hind leg caught your eye, you are not alone. His reach and extension surpasses the correct but less dramatic diagonal action of the Borzoi. This is because

The Dalmatian, Smooth Fox Terrier, Wire Fox Terrier, Dachshund and the Borzoi

this Dalmatian is wrongly supported on only his right front leg. This single support suggests a front with rear imbalance and, that instead of diagonal feet relinquishing support together, each foot relinquishes support independently. This imbalance is partly responsible for this Dalmatian's over-reach, I say partly because he may have been moving too fast.

The Smooth Fox Terrier was also captured on film supported on just one leg and it appears that he will also be forced to over-reach. What has happened is that this Terrier was photographed not at a full trot but at the moment he was pulled to an abrupt stop. There is a good chance this dog is sound and balanced.

In addition to using a fast shutter speed and shooting at a low eye level, the dog must be moving at his best speed, be moving at right angles to the camera at the moment the picture is taken, travel always from right to left as in the show ring, start the trot 20 feet to the right of camera, and finish trot 20 feet to the left to ensure smoothness at critical moment. Also take many photographs.

The photograph of this Wire Fox Terrier captured diagonal legs correctly relinquishing support (lift) together, suggesting that this dog is balanced front with rear. But his leg positions cannot be used to depict good movement because he evidences a serious structural fault. This Wire is sickle-hocked.

A number of breeds have problems with hocks that do not fully open. The term sickle-hocked is taken from the short-handled, semi-circular blade used for lopping or trimming farm produce, much in the shape of this Wire's left hind leg. This Wire's left hind hock at this stage should be open and the foot positioned rearward of where it is now. The dog's left hind pastern (leg between hock and foot) might eventually extend rearward to a vertical position, but no further.

A dog with a hind pastern that cannot open is unable to exert thrust rearward when the foot is on the ground, or to continue to extend the hind leg rearward on the follow-through. To compensate for reduced rearward extension some dogs will over-lift the hind leg bringing it forward in a high, rotary fashion.

This sickle-hocked Dachshund with too long a hind pastern adopts a different way to compensate for not being able to extend the left hind foot rearward beyond the vertical position of the hind pastern. To extend the time the hind foot should be off the ground she is "goose stepping" with her right hind leg. This hind leg energy-wasteful departure is the source of the term "tummy thumper."

In summary, selecting the best photograph to advertise a dog's movement at the trot requires three particular actions to look for among the dozens of photographs taken. In terms of dramatic presentation, the most impressive will be when all four feet are off the ground. Second will be at the moment diagonal feet strike the ground together. Third will be at the moment diagonal feet relinquish support (lift) together.

In the photograph you select, the dog must be supported on two diagonal legs or none. If supported only on one leg the dog was moving too fast, was coming to a stop, or is not balanced front with rear. If supported on two legs—but not two diagonal legs—the dog's forward travel was restricted in some way (e.g. tight lead), or he was coming to a stop when the photograph was taken.

More and more advertisers are promoting their sound dogs captured on film moving at the trot in a correct manner and more and more readers are aware that unsoundness is the reason why, in some published photographs, the dog is supported on one leg. In addition, more and more Illustrated Guide Committees are directing their artists as to how good movement at the trot should be depicted.

CHAPTER TWENTY-TWO
EIGHT TROTTING STYLES

While not all breeds are endurance trotters and there is no such a thing as a universal trot, there is a trot that is common to many breeds. A good moving Golden Retriever would serve to represent this norm. In addition to this common style there are at least seven more recognized trotting styles that you should be aware of. Some are described in their Breed Standard in detail, others less so, some not at all. Judges who are not aware of or not knowledgeable of these styles can put these breeds at a disadvantage when evaluating gait.

The Ibizan Hound

Function often dictates the manner in which a breed will trot. The Ibizan Hound is a classic example. A Sighthound capable of a second period of suspension at the fast gallop, the Ibizan Hound also moves in a distinctive manner at the trot.

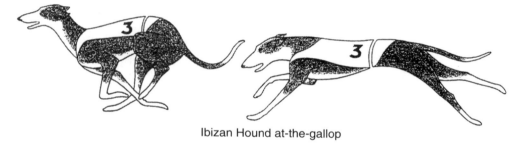

Ibizan Hound at-the-gallop

This unique breed derives its name from Ibiza, a Spanish Island that has been ruled by Egyptians, Arabs, Carthaginians, Romans, Chaldeans, and Vandals. Isolated for hundreds of years, the breed has adapted very well. Unlike most Sighthounds, the Ibizan can hunt by sound as well as sight and scent. His appearance is as unusual as his talents.

Ibizans

Before discussing the way in which the Ibizan departs from the norm I have provided three Ibizan Hounds for your selection of first, second and third. Their appearances differ in ways that relate to function. Which Ibizan do you believe is the more typical?

Did you have trouble deciding that the best Ibizan is Dog B? Dog A is too heavy in neck, body and bone. Dog C is long in both ribcage and loin; the body should be only slightly longer than height.

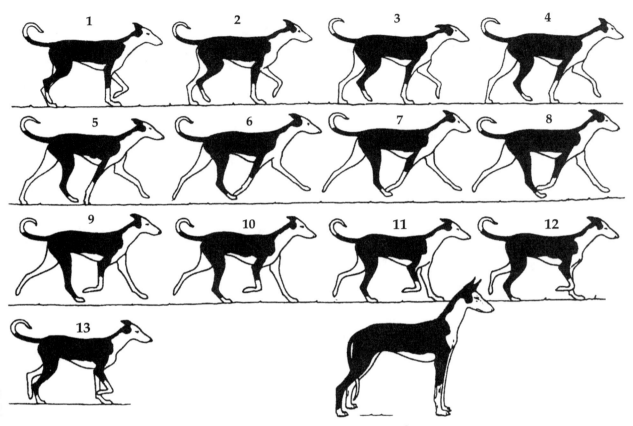

Ibizan Hound at the Trot: An Illustrated Sequence

Now for gait. The Ibizan Hound is built for speed and agility. However, it is at the trot that he is judged. You should be aware that at the trot this breed displays a unique "hovering" gait as in Phase 7 of the Illustrated Sequence where the forefoot tends to hover before being placed on the ground.

The Chow Chow

An ancient breed of northern Chinese origin, this all-purpose dog of China was used for hunting, herding, pulling and protection of the home. While primarily a companion today, his working origin must always be remembered when assessing true Chow type. He is a powerful, sturdy, squarely built, upstanding dog of Arctic type — medium in size, with strong muscular development, and heavy bone. The body is compact, short coupled, broad and deep, the tail set high and carried close to the back, the whole supported by four straight, strong sound legs. Viewed from the side the hind legs have little apparent angulation, and the hock joint and metatarsals are directly beneath the hip joint. It is this structure that produces the characteristic short, stilted gait unique to the breed.

Chow Chows move at the trot in a unique manner seldom seen to perfection. The dog must be sound, straight moving, agile, brief, quick and powerful, never lumbering. The rear gait is short and stilted in the manner exhibited by Dog A because of the straighter rear assembly. Compare correctly constructed Dog A with the greater amount of angulation possessed by the average dog shown in Dog B. It is from the side that the unique stilted action is most easily assessed. The rear leg moves up and forward from the hip in a straight, stilted

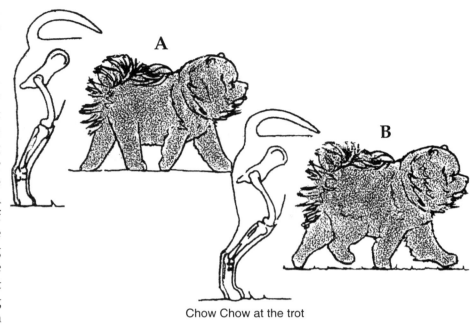

Chow Chow at the trot

(swinging as if on stilts) pendulum-like action with a slight bounce in the rump. The legs extend neither far forward nor far backward nor does the hind leg bend at stifle and hock in the manner of Dog B. The hind foot has a strong thrust that transfers power directly to the body in an almost straight line due to the minimal rear leg angulation. To transmit this power efficiently to the front assembly, the coupling must be short and there should be no roll through the midsection.

The Fox Terrier

The Fox Terrier's action at the trot differs from that of endurance trotters because he — like the Wire, Airedale, Lakeland, Irish, and Welsh Terriers — has a similar, distinctive digging front, one with a well laid-back shoulder, a short rather perpendicular upper arm, and very little forechest or slope to front pastern.

The AKC Fox Terrier Standard describes gait in a seemingly conflicting paragraph. Conflicting because it informs that movement is crucial then suggests imbalance by asking for the hindquarters to provide the principle propulsive power. This direction in the Standard is used by some exhibitors to justify lifting the front off the floor by means of a tight lead. In asking for the hindquarters

Airedale Terrier and Smooth Fox Terrier

to provide the principal propulsion power the Standard may be referring to the Fox Terrier's ability to keep up with horse and fox at-the-gallop — not the trot. Bill Dosset, a long-time Fox Terrier breeder, writes in the AKC Gazette March 1994, "Poor movement showed up in dogs with good rear structure but not so good front carriage…if you look at the landing pattern of the front and rear feet of the properly structured Fox Terrier, you will see that the rear foot lands a mere half inch behind the front foot." Coming, the feet of these terriers (in this case an Airedale) travel forward the same distance apart as the elbows. In profile below, the reach forward and extension rearward of the legs of the Smooth Fox Terrier is that of an earth digger, not an endurance trotter like the Dalmatian.

Dalmatian and Smooth Fox Terrier at the trot

The Dachshund

One of these two Dachshunds standing and moving straight on is correctly constructed while the other is not. Which is correct?

The Dachshund's unorthodox digging front differs from the norm in that the elbow positions well above the deepest part of the brisket. The elbow on most breeds is level with the deepest part of the brisket. Viewed from the front, the shoulder blades are closely positioned at the withers. The elbow positions well above the bottom of the chest and the forearm between the elbow and the wrist curves slightly around the low-slung body. This brings the wrists in slightly closer than the points of the shoulders on the correct example. The foreleg on correct Dog A is straight only from the wrist down. His feet are correctly inclined a trifle outward. This style of wrap-around front produces a smoother, more controlled action coming than the incorrect short upper arm and straight front on Dog B.

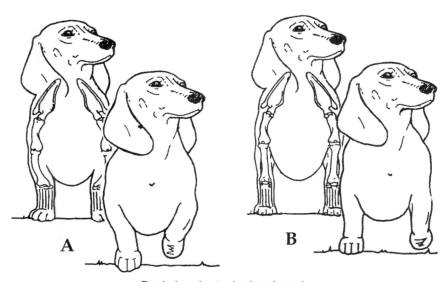

A   B

Dachshunds stacked and moving

121

The German Shepherd

A properly constructed German Shepherd moves with the smooth powerful, steady motion of a well lubricated machine. To appreciate the German Shepherd's outreaching, elastic, seeming without effort action at the flying trot, I have placed him beside a more moderately angulated Belgian Tervuren. The difference in reach and over-reach is apparent. The over-reach of the German Shepherd in the Illustrated Sequence is not faulty unless the locomotion is crabwise, (i.e. the dog's body not being carried forward in a straight line).

The German Shepherd and the Tervuren have legs that incline slightly inward toward the center of the body to maintain balance. The Tervuren is one of the few breeds whose inner toes touch a center line under the body. The Belgian Malinois, the Belgian Sheepdog, the Collie, and the Shetland Sheepdog are four more.

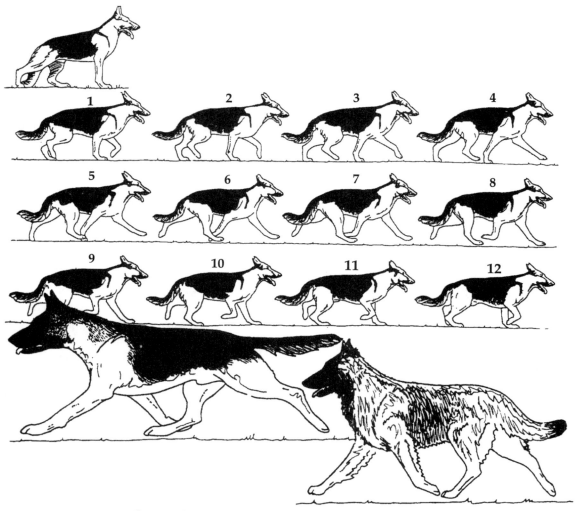

German Shepherd at the trot and the single track of the Belgian Tervuren

The Golden Retriever

This Golden Retriever stacked and moving in profile represents the norm in the canine world — the endurance trotter. May I draw your attention to Phases 5 and 6 where during the change-over of diagonals there is a brief period of suspension, all four feet free of contact with the ground. It is this phase that should be employed when movement is limited to a single drawing.

Endurance trotters are usually slightly longer than tall with a length of leg equal to depth of body. The best canine mover I have on film is this Golden Retriever. Notice that the diagonal legs relinquish support together as a pair, then strike the ground together, and lastly there is a brief period of suspension during the change-over. All four legs are reaching out and extending rearward an equal distance.

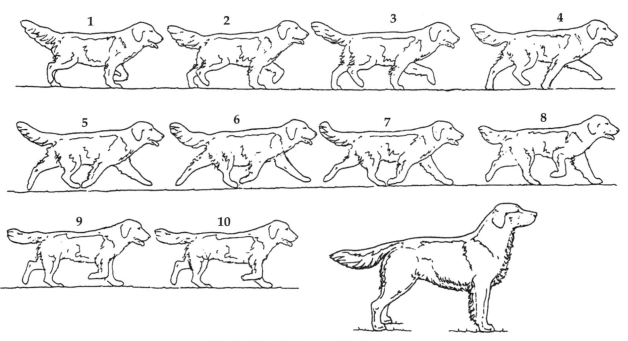

The Golden Retriever at the trot

The Bulldog

Because of its unorthodox conformation, the Bulldog moves in an unorthodox fashion — not so much coming as going away. Which of the two Bulldogs in the next drawings are moving correctly coming and going?

Coming the Bulldog's front legs should converge slightly, be carried straight forward and the feet point straight ahead at the trot as in the case of Dog A.

Stacked, the front feet may be straight or slightly turned out. From the rear, the stifles on Dog D turn outward, away from the body forcing the hocks to approach each other. The other Bulldog's hindquarters have been set wider apart by an exhibitor who is not aware that cowhocks are not a fault in this breed. This is a common occurrence. The exhibitor wants to improve the appearance of the hindquarters by straightening the cowhocks and in doing so produces a departure from type.

The Bulldog stacked, from the rear—which is correct?

The Bulldog coming and going—which is correct?

My attempt to depict action going away is made necessary because it is essential to know that the hind leg must get by a body wider in front than behind. This is why the stifles turn out and the hocks turn in and why the hind leg is brought forward around the supporting leg in a semi-circular fashion. The "characteristic roll" is the result of this unusual action as I have illustrated here. Based on this information and these illustrations it should be clear that Bulldog D is correct.

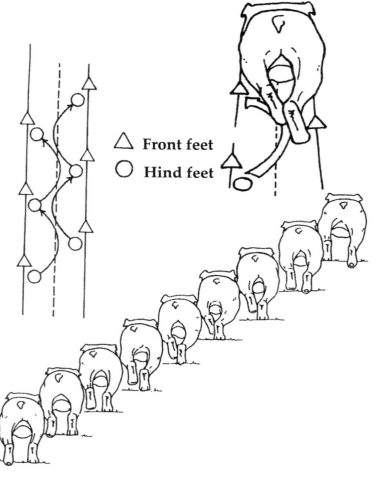

△ **Front feet**

○ **Hind feet**

The Bulldog going away

The Miniature Pinscher

One of the five Miniature Pinschers is moving correctly for this Toy breed. Which one? All five have been drawn from illustrated sequences filmed at 54 frames per second. All five exhibit different action in Phase 2, the most informative phase for this particular breed. In Phase 2 the front leg is lifted dramatically but wastefully high. In addition there are a number of other action features to take into account in deciding which Min Pin best represents movement at the trot typical for this breed.

The Miniature Pinscher Standard requires a "hackney" or "hackney-like" gait. The Canadian Min Pin Standard requires "precise hackney gait." Britain asks for a movement to "coordinate to permit a true hackneyed action." United States modifies the requirement by asking for "hackney-like action," however it elaborates on other important aspects such as wrist bend.

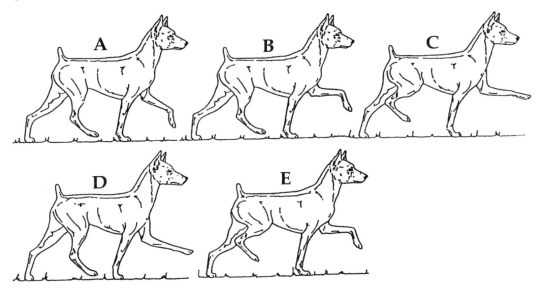

Five different Miniature Pinschers in Phase 2 at the Trot

Requirement for bend at the wrist in the expanded American Standard (1980) reads: "The hackney-like action is a high-stepping, reaching, free and easy gait in which the front leg moves straight forward and in front of the body and the foot bends at the wrist. The dog drives smoothly and strongly from the rear. The head and tail are carried high."

Because hackney action is usually a fault in most breeds caused by steep shoulders, many people believe a Min Pin must have steep shoulders to exhibit this energy-wasteful but aesthetically pleasing hackney action. The reverse is true, however not all writers agree. The late Harry Spira in his illustrated textbook *Canine Terminology*, added fuel to the debate with his statement that: "Min Pin hackney action requires rather steep shoulder angulation, coupled with upright pasterns,"

None of the three Standards specifically require the hind leg to also lift high but the British Standard does so indirectly by requiring that movement be "coordinated to permit true hackneyed action." To be coordinated diagonal feet lift and strike the ground together as pairs, therefore the hind leg must also lift high and remain free of contact with the ground the same length of time as the diagonal front foot. Also, to lift the hind leg high, the belly must be moderately tucked up, a requirement in every Min Pin Standard.

If you selected moderately angulated front and rear Dog E as typical we are in accord. His hind leg bends at stifle and his hock is lifted high, his forearm is raised to horizontal and the wrist is bent. My second place is sound Dog A. His action is desired of most breeds. He is balanced front with rear but lacks dramatic hackney action. I awarded third place to steep-shouldered Dog B because although he goose steps high in front and does not bend his wrist, he does hackney in rear. Fourth place goes to steep-shouldered C. He goose steps in front (often mistaken for hackney) and fails to bend at the wrist. He also fails to bend and raise his hind leg, a failure that often goes unnoticed.

This Illustrated Sequence depicts typical Min Pin action at the trot in profile that is similar to that of most dogs with the exception of Phase 2, where the diagonal right rear and left front legs lift very high. The action is rapid, however awareness of the period of suspension and that diagonal feet lift and strike the ground together as pairs aids in seeing gait.

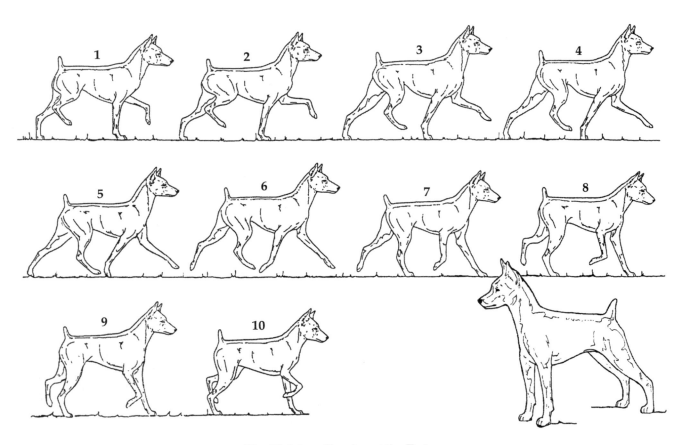

The Miniature Pinscher at the Trot

CHAPTER TWENTY-THREE
THE FOX TROT

There are six Terrier breeds that, due to their specialized forequarters, do not move at the trot in the same manner as normally constructed breeds. These six Terrier breeds shown below are: the Airedale, the Lakeland, the Smooth Fox Terrier, the Wire Fox Terrier, the Irish Terrier, and the Welsh Terrier.

Six Terrier breeds with specialized forequarters. Clockwise from the top left: Lakeland Terrier, Welsh Terrier, Wirehair Fox Terrier, Smooth Fox Terrier, Airedale Terrier, Irish Terrier.

This illustrated treatise describes the form this specialized Terrier structure takes, compares it to a more normal structure, and then compares the distinctly different trotting action of this specialized digging Terrier to the action of an endurance trotting breed. I chose the Smooth Fox Terrier to represent the specialized digging structure possessed by all six of these Terrier breeds and the equally smooth Dalmatian to represent the normal structure as possessed by many endurance-trotting breeds.

Specialized Terrier vs. Normal Structure

Let's begin with structural similarities stacked in profile. Both breeds have well laid-back shoulder blades, straight forearms, forelegs equal in length to depth of body, elbows level with brisket, level toplines, moderate tuck-up, a shelf over the buttocks, moderate hindquarter angulation, and short rear pasterns. The most important structural difference influencing function, balance and locomotion readily observed in profile between this Fox Terrier and this Dalmatian is the length and angle of the upper arm (the humerus).

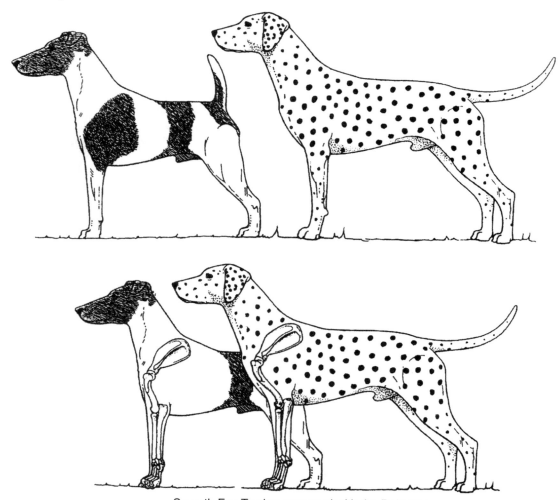

Smooth Fox Terrier compared with the Dalmatian

The Dalmatian is intended for endurance at the trot over long distance. To accomplish this the length of body from forechest to buttocks is about 10 percent longer than height at the withers, the topline is level except for a slight arch over the loin, the foreleg is the same length as the body from withers to brisket is deep, the tail comes off level with the spine, the elbow is level with the bottom of the chest, the bone is medium in weight, and angulation is good front and rear. By contrast the Fox Terrier is intended for going to ground not for endurance trotting. The body measures about the same length from forechest to buttocks as height from withers to ground. The level back is short, the loin muscular and very slightly arched, the tail is set on rather high and carried gaily, and the forequarters are quite different from the Dalmatian.

Forequarters

In this cut-away of the Dalmatian's forequarters, the sloping upper arm is revealed to be about the same length as the shoulder blade which in turn positions the elbow well rearward on the body. This oblique angle of shoulder blade and upper arm provides for a good forechest. To complete static balance, the Dalmatian's front pastern slopes slightly forward, positioning the foot directly under the center of support. This is conducive to endurance at the trot and so the forequarter assembly differs greatly from that of the Fox Terrier.

The Fox Terrier's upper arm differs from the norm in that it is both shorter and has a steeper angle. This shortness and steepness of the upper arm positions the foreleg forward on the body and reduces degree of forechest, changes the location of the elbow and forces the front pastern to position vertical so that the front foot is more under the center of forequarter support. This shortening and steepening of the upper arm permits the arc of the elbow to move forward and back above the brisket line, a distinct advantage when the dog goes to ground to bolt the fox. As for appearance, Terrier breeders of old aimed for an almost vertical line from in front of the neck right down to the toes with almost no projection of forechest. This straight line produces a very alert, up-on-the-toes appearance at the expense of reach at the trot.

Trot In Profile

I have positioned the Dalmatian ahead of the Smooth Fox Terrier in a single-phase action drawing at the trot, the Dalmatian having the greater reach. This single phase is where, during the process of changing from one pair of diagonals to the opposite pair, the motion picture camera has captured the brief period of suspension where the body is projected forward, all four feet free of contact with the ground.

Both dogs are well balanced front and rear and their respective diagonal feet will strike the ground together as a pair. Over the complete cycle there will be either two diagonal feet or no feet on the ground at any given moment. I am pleased that in the latest revision to the AKC Dalmatian Standard the incorrect advice that "the gait should be steady in rhythm of 1, 2, 3, 4, as in the cadence of military drill" was deleted. Soldiers march on two feet, dogs trot on four. A Dalmatian that exhibited a four-time beat in which each foot struck the ground independently suggests a front-to-rear imbalance.

Smooth Fox Terrier compared with the Dalmatian at the trot

Both breeds have the same good length and layback of shoulder blade. However, the Dalmatian has greater reach. The reason for the Dalmatian's greater reach of the front leg at the trot is a longer length of upper arm. To specialize at going to ground the Fox Terrier and the other five Terriers (although the Airedale is somewhat large for this task) possess a short, steep upper arm and this is what restricts forward reach.

As for official requirements for upper arms both short and steep or restricted action, don't bother looking for it in the Standards for these six terriers for you will not find it. Either terrier breeders of old took it for granted that we knew what they intended or they thought that the front legs of all breeds "swing like the pendulum of a clock." The reference to the "swing" was deleted in 1986 from the British Standard (sadly deleted in the opinion of the late Tom Horner), but it tells a great deal about the Terrier trot and what to look for. First, don't look for the forward reach you would expect on a Dalmatian or a Kerry Blue Terrier. Second, be prepared to find feet carried forward and back very close to the ground (called "Daisy clipping"). Third, do not be surprised that the front pastern hardly flexes at the wrist (compare the drawing to the maximum horizontal flex of the Dalmatian's front pastern).

There are, however, two indirect clues to the promotion of a short, steep upper arm in all Fox Terrier Standards. The first is that "the elbows should hang perpendicular to the body" and the second is that "the forelegs should be straight right down to the feet, being short and straight in pastern." In other words, the elbow positions forward on the body nearly under the point of shoulder and there is no slope to the front pastern when stacked, resulting in hardly any flex of the front pastern at the trot.

Under the Body

In the previous illustration the Dalmatian's right hind foot is shown slipping under the flexed right front foot to occupy the spot vacated by the latter. Not so with the Fox Terrier. Under the body in the correctly structured Fox Terrier, the right hind foot cannot slip under the right front foot because the right hind foot doesn't reach forward enough nor does the left front foot extend far enough rearward for this to happen. Besides, the right front pastern does not flex high enough for the right hind foot to slip under it even if it did reach that far forward.

Based on visual observation of slow-motion film, it appears the hind foot of well-made Smooth Fox Terrier A does not occupy the spot vacated by the front foot, rather, the hind foot lands about a half inch behind it. This is also the landing pattern distance decided upon as correct for the properly structured Fox Terrier by researcher Bill Dossett of New River, Arizona. When the distance between the front foot and the hind foot on the same side is greater than a half inch, the body is either too long, there is insufficient angulation front and rear, the legs are too short, or the hindquarters are superior to the forequarters caused by steep and often short shoulder blades.

Unfortunately, the current AKC and CKC Fox Terrier Standards suggest a requirement for a superior hindquarter to forequarter, front-to-rear imbalance by advising, "The principal propulsive power is furnished by the hind legs." This advice may be the reason many exhibitors are obliged to "carry" their Fox Terriers with weak fronts on a tight lead as with Dog B. In 1986, five years before the current AKC and

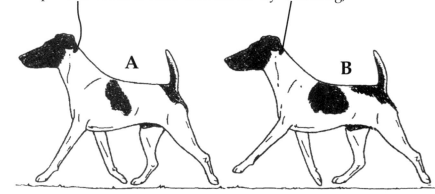

Smooth Fox Terriers at the trot

CKC Standards were revised, the British deleted promotion of front-to-rear imbalance and went instead with "good drive coming from well flexing hindquarters."

Face-On Stacked and Moving

Smooth Fox Terrier and Dalmatian stacked face-on

The intent of this face-on drawing of the Smooth Fox Terrier and a Dalmatian is to contrast respective breadth of body and the effect of breadth and structure on action at the trot coming.

The Fox Terrier's body should be somewhat narrow rather than broad whereas the Dalmatian's body, although not as broad as the Bull Terrier is broad, is broader than the Fox Terrier. This in turn means the Fox Terrier's forelegs are set closer together than the Dalmatian's. Add to this that the Fox Terrier's upper arm is shorter and steeper and the result is an action coming that is quite different from that of the Dalmatian.

The Dalmatian's endurance trotting structure causes the front legs, at the speed moved in the show ring, to tend to converge toward a single line under the center of the body for maximum stability. The faster this dog is trotted the more convergence there will be. The Fox Terrier's go-to-ground structure causes the front legs to travel straight forward, parallel to each other. In other words, coming, the feet travel the same distance apart as the elbows.

So while a shortened upper arm is a serious structure fault for most breeds, it is a requirement for six Terriers: the Airedale, the Lakeland, the Smooth Fox Terrier, the Wire Fox Terrier, the Irish Terrier, and the Welsh Terrier.

Airedale and Smooth Fox Terrier have shortened upper arm structure

CHAPTER TWENTY-FOUR
THE FLYING TROT

The German Shepherd

The German Shepherd flying trot is one of the most beautiful but least understood of the canine gaits. Beauty is in the reach and extension, a long period of suspension where all four feet are free of contact with the ground, over-reach of the hind legs past the front leg without crabbing and the level, seemingly without effort, close-to-the-ground action.

To lessen misunderstanding I have provided two Illustrated Sequences at the trot, one of a good German Shepherd stacked and moving in profile and the other of a dog resembling the German Shepherd of 50 years ago, but one still with us today.

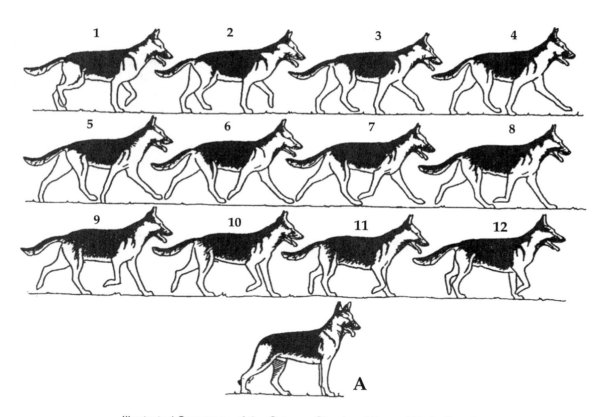

Illustrated Sequence of the German Shepherd Normal Trot - Dog A

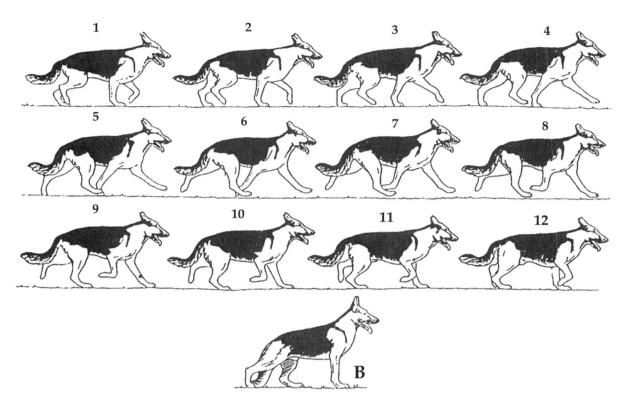

Illustrated Sequence of the German Shepherd Flying Trot - Dog B

I trust you did not have too much difficulty deciding which one of these two Open Class German Shepherds would win. Deciding the winner was easy. Now comes the question: What are the four major differences between the action of the more angulated Dog B at the flying trot, and the action of old-fashioned Dog A at the normal trot? Traced from slow-motion movie film, these two illustrated sequences permit phase-by-phase comparison between two different but sound German Shepherds. It is possible, using this illustrated comparison format, to identify all four major locomotion differences. What are they?

A Closer Look

The four major differences between the greater angulated Dog B and Dog A are: (1) longer period of suspension; (2) over-reaching under his body; (3) a lower profile; and (4) a longer stride. Other than that, the action at the flying trot shown by dog B is similar to moderately angulated dog A at the Normal Trot. Both have a diagonal, two-beat gait tempos.

Both the normal trot and the flying trot have a two-beat gait tempo, i.e., one pair of diagonals strike the ground together, then the second pair of diagonals strike the ground together — two beats for each cycle. Old-fashioned Dog A's diagonal left hind and right front feet strike together in Phase 8. More angulated Dog B's same diagonal feet strike together one phase later in Phase 9 because his period of suspension, where all four feet are off the ground, is longer.

Some German Shepherd fanciers believe that theirs is the only breed that exhibits a period of suspension at the trot, but they are wrong. Slow-motion photography has proven that all breeds exhibit varying degrees of suspension where all four feet are free of contact with the ground at the trot. Old-fashioned Dog A represents action at the normal trot of moderately angulated, normally constructed breeds capable of covering distance at this least tiring trot.

To appreciate that all dogs must exhibit a brief period of suspension at the normal trot, note that if moderately angulated Dog A's four feet were not off the ground during change-over of diagonals in Phases 6 and 7, his right hind foot could not slip smoothly underneath his right front foot without interference. The second reason for suspension is that an airborne period lengthens a dog's stride. The third reason for suspension is to allow time (swing-time) for the legs to be carried fully forward.

Greater angulated Dog B's longer period of suspension is due to his faster speed. He needs to be airborne longer to allow his legs enough swing-time. This faster speed necessitates the over-reaching of his legs under his body.

All normally constructed breeds will break from the normal trot into the Flying Trot if moved too fast. However, when they do, over-reach occurs under their bodies and this action usually causes them to crab. The current German Shepherd is designed to over-reach at the fast Flying Trot without crabbing (a side, crab-like action seen going away shown below).

Greater angulated Dog B over-reaches in Phases 5, 6, and 7. If this dog's right hind foot did not over-reach past the right front foot during these phases, interference would occur. This would cause most breeds to crab but not the German Shepherd. The current ideal German Shepherd is built to avoid crabbing. To avoid crabbing, this dog's right hind foot passes on the outside of the right front foot, and in the second half of the cycle his left hind foot passes on the inside of the left front foot. Seen going away this action is not faulty unless locomotion is crabwise with the dog's body moving sideways out of the normal straight line.

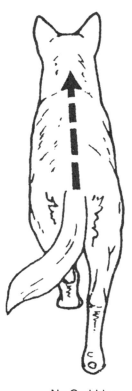

The typical German Shepherd presents a low profile at the flying trot. Once seen to perfection it is never forgotten. In order to produce this low profile (the topline level and firm) and desired gliding effect, the leg joints fold excessively. Long reach and extension of all four legs with maximum bending of joints is demanded. The end product is a spectacular, smooth, seemingly without effort action, beautiful to watch, a pleasure to judge.

The German Shepherd is a trotting dog, and its structure has been developed to

No Crabbing   Crabbing

meet the requirements of its work. Its stride (the distance covered in one cycle) is the maximum distance that can be covered with the minimum number of steps. To accomplish this, all four legs reach fully forward, the forelegs reaching out close to the ground to produce a long stride in harmony with that of balanced hindquarters.

Awareness that both the flying trot and the normal trot are diagonal two-beat gaits with a period of suspension during change-over of diagonals, and that there are either two feet or no feet on the ground at any given time, prepares the eye to "see" movement, regardless of breed.

"Seeing" the German Shepherd's action at the flying trot only requires you take over-reach, a longer period of suspension, a low profile, and a long stride into consideration.

PART IV

FAULTS AND ILLUSIONS

CHAPTER TWENTY-FIVE
WHEN FAULTS ARE PROMOTED

When judging, care must be taken not to promote faults — or to condemn faults that are in fact a virtue. Often the knowledge that is needed about the feature in question requires study beyond the published guidelines. Let's look at several examples in this chapter.

The Collie

Two of these Collies have correct breed conformation. Which two? Be sure you do not mistakenly condemn a hindquarter fault that should be viewed as a virtue. The AKC Seminar paper titled *Observations…Hocks and Stifles* by John Buddie has a diagram of this feature accompanied by text as does the 1961 *Illustrations of the Collie, His Character and Conformation* by Lorraine B. Still.

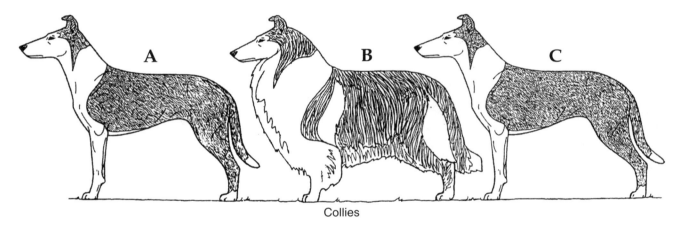

Collies

Anyone tasked with judging this herding breed should have sufficient knowledge of what sets the Collie's balance apart so that the feature in question will not be mistaken for a fault. The feature in question is the position of the hind leg standing as seen in profile. The hind leg should be more under the body than exhibited by Collie C. Collie A and Collie B are correct according to Still's diagram which has a line dropped down from the point of buttocks to the front of the rear pastern. Buddie advises that "The rear pasterns are set slightly rear of the pelvis."

Covered with a profuse coat, Rough Collie B's distinctive balance is due to having the same moderately angulated hindquarters as Smooth Collie A. Granted, hind legs are only one feature, but from a functional standpoint, it is an important one. Let me quote another expert, "The Collie's gait suggests effortless speed combined with the dog's herding heritage, requiring it to be capable of changing direction of travel almost instantaneously." Vertical rear pasterns that position further back than Collies A and B are less likely to possess these capabilities.

The Pointer

This next dog is taken from a seminar video clip that I have used successfully to illustrate loss of breed type. Pointer A should remind you of another breed—a German Shorthaired Pointer. Pointer A should never serve as an example of typical. It is important that a judge has a clear picture in his mind's eye of a good Pointer.

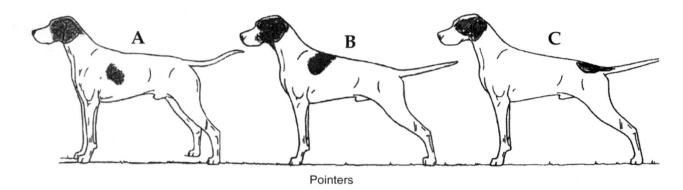

Pointers

Pointer C is a good Pointer and serves to represent typical. Pointer B is a good German Shorthaired Pointer. Pointer A resembles more the good German Shorthaired Pointer than he does the good Pointer. When a judge carries a flawed image of typical into the ring, faults are often promoted as virtues.

The Bullmastiff

Breeds are readily identified by their heads. You cannot mistake a Bullmastiff's head for that of another breed, however within this breed there are a large variety of faces, due partly to the happy blend of Bulldog and Mastiff. So not only does the head identify the breed, it must also possess pleasing facial characteristics. In the case of the Bullmastiff — like the facial differences in a race of men — the number of different faces are almost limitless, some handsome, some not so. Deciding what is handsome for a Bullmastiff is an interesting challenge.

In what order of "handsome" would you place these three champion heads, each having identical bodies, and in what way(s) would you improve on each head?

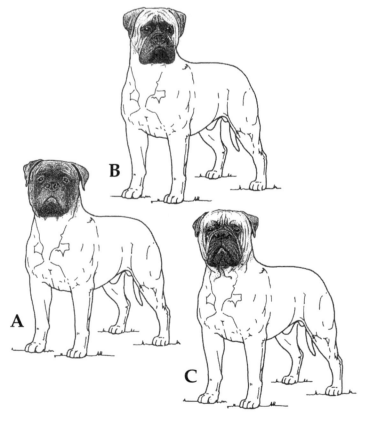

Bullmastiffs

Would it help to read/reread the section on head? The 1992 Standard reads,

> HEAD — Expression, keen, alert and intelligent.
>
> EYES — Dark and of medium size.
>
> EARS — V-shaped and carried close to the cheeks, set on wide and high, level with the occiput and cheeks, giving a square appearance to the skull, darker in color than the body and medium size.
>
> SKULL — Large, with a fair amount of wrinkle when alert: broad, with cheeks well developed. Forehead Flat.
>
> STOP — Moderate.
>
> MUZZLE — Broad and deep; its length, in comparison with that of the entire head, approximately as 1 is to 3. Lack of foreface with nostrils set on top of muzzle is a reversion to the Bulldog and is very undesirable. A dark muzzle is preferable.
>
> NOSE — Black, with nostrils large and broad.
>
> FLEWS — Not too pendulous.
>
> BITE — Preferably level or slightly undershot. Canine teeth large and set well apart.
>
> STANDARD EXPANDED — No Bullmastiff Standard describes the shape of the dark eye nor do available books on the breed except for Douglas F. Olliff's *The Mastiff and Bullmastiff Handbook* which describes the eye as almond shaped. In addition, the broad muzzle should sustain almost the same width to the end of the nose, the underjaw should be broad to the end, and the eyes should be spaced well apart.

This written blueprint of the Bullmastiff head plus expansion is of little value read in isolation unless it is studied in conjunction with real-life heads. These three real-life heads, although far from ideal, help formulate an image of ideal and at the same time lessen the likelihood that the Bullmastiff head virtues will be seen as faults. Consider placing these three heads in order of merit after or before you decide what features you would change in the pursuit of an ideal.

Dog A's round skull should be made square and the ears should be brought forward, made smaller, and their inner edge made to lie close to the cheek. The broad muzzle is impressive as is the strong underjaw. The cheeks should be better developed and the looseness at the neck tightened. The loose eye rims also need tightening and the eyes made almond shaped. The cheeks have too much wrinkle and the flews are too heavy (long).

Dog B's ears are too large and set on too close together at the top of the skull. Eyes should be spaced further apart and eye rims tightened. Loose cheek wrinkles should be spaced further apart and eye rims tightened. Muzzle should be made a little broader at top.

With Dog C, the profuse cheek wrinkles should be eliminated and the cheeks and jawbones should be better defined under the cheeks. The eyes are okay and the muzzle has breadth, however some of the flews should be removed as well as the loose throat tissue.

I gave head C first place, head A second and head B third.

The Labrador Retriever

Prior to AKC approval of the Labrador Standard in 1994, any one of these three yellow Labs might be considered typical. Now under the 1994 revised guideline only one of these three examples has correct Lab conformation. Decide which one is correct then place the other two.

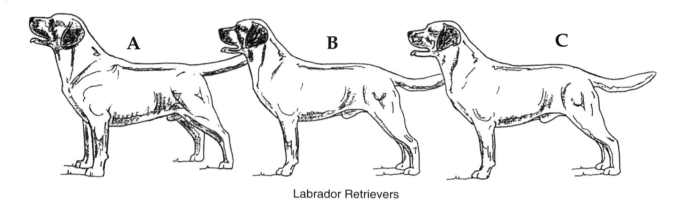

Labrador Retrievers

The sentence in the 1994 revision that determines that only one of these three Labs is correctly proportioned reads, "Distance from the elbow to the ground should be equal to one half the height at the withers. The brisket should extend to the elbows, but not perceptibly deeper" and, "short-legged individuals are not typical of the breed."

Lab A's body is too deep, the brisket below the elbow. Lab C is short legged. Lab B represents typical. I placed Lab A second and Lab C third. Knowing that the elbow should be positioned half the height to the withers, and the brisket be level with the elbow, ensures that a brisket incorrectly deeper than the elbow, or a dog with a short leg, will not be promoted. As mentioned earlier, when a judge carries a flawed image of typical into the ring, the right faults can easily be promoted as virtues.

CHAPTER TWENTY-SIX
MINIMIZING FAULTS

Minimizing faults is fair game. The exhibitor should present his or her imperfect dog to the dog's best advantage. Judges, some of whom may have utilized the same means when exhibiting dogs, need to try to see past subterfuge to find the true dog.

The Basenji

Which of these two Basenjis stacked in profile is sounder? Both stacks were filmed on the same day, on the same table, and moving in profile as you will see later in this chapter. At this point you are invited to compare Dog A and Bitch B stacked and decide which one you prefer and why.

If you decided in favor of sounder Dog A, you are probably aware of the two faults the cunning exhibitor could not hide on Bitch B and wondered about a third — regardless of the means used by the exhibitor to minimize these faults. Are you aware of what the exhibitor has done to improve Bitch B's appearance? Regardless of the subterfuge can you identify the two faults, one in the forequarters area and the other in the loin area?

Basenjis, Dog A and Bitch B

Bitch B's first fault is a long loin helped made visible by the white line defining the positioning of the last rib. The second fault is steepness in the forequarter area. The exhibitor has done a very good job of stacking this unsound Basenji but is unable to line up the elbow with the brisket. Since the body possesses the required depth and the upper arm is of correct length, the fault must be a steep upper arm, the elbow positioning below the brisket.

By luck I chanced to film unsound Bitch B on the table in a natural stack and then a second later in an improved stack shown in the illustration on the next page. The exhibitor in one smooth motion had improved Bitch B by simply moving the hind feet two inches rearward and then by exerting forward pressure with two fingers at the base of the tail. The improvement to appearance was and is dramatic.

In the "before" stack of the next illustration there is an obvious dip in the topline due in part to the long, unsupported loin. The second thigh could be longer, or the upper thigh, or both. The front pastern could have less slope and the forequarters should not be so far forward on the body. The too high carriage of the head doesn't help to produce a forechest and suggests a less than desirable shoulder angulation.

Aside from a low below-the-brisket elbow position, most of these faults have been minimized in the "after" stack. Of course, the rear pasterns are no longer vertical but this form of subterfuge often goes unnoticed even in win photographs.

Important as the view going away and coming is, the view in profile tells a much fuller story. The view in profile discloses: the degree of up and down and levelness of the topline; the carriage of the neck and head; the reach and extension of all four legs; the degree of front pastern flex; synchronized diagonal footfalls; and the means an unsound dog may utilize to attain a degree of balance front to rear.

Basenji Bitch B, before and after an adjustment on the table

Now let's compare action at the trot in profile of these two Basenjis illustrated on the next page. To enable you to compare phase-by-phase the action of two differently constructed dogs, each illustrated sequence begins with the right front leg in vertical support. The position of the other three legs will vary depending on how well the dog is constructed. The dog at the trot will serve as the norm for this breed.

Bitch B shows imbalance front with rear, as captured early in Phase 1, the too far advanced right hind leg being a giveaway. Notice that the left hind leg, rather than supporting in Phase 1, is actually exerting rearward pressure. The topline slopes down toward a low-carried head and the left front leg is lifted wastefully high. Because of this imbalance the diagonal left hind leg and right front leg in Phase 3 do not relinquish support at the same time — the right front leg is still in a support mode. This one front leg support ironically allows the left front leg to reach further forward than her steep shoulders would normally permit.

Even though in Phase 4 the hind legs lack angulation, the right hind foot, because of the poor timing, must over-reach past the delayed right front to avoid interference. Although premature and of a very short duration there is still a very brief period of suspension. The period of suspension is cut short in Phase 5 when the left front foot strikes the ground before the diagonal right hind foot. The beat is four-time rather than the required two-time beat for a complete cycle. Because of the lowness of the front and the poor timing, the right hind foot in Phase 5 is unable to slip neatly under the flexed right front foot and occupy the spot vacated by the latter.

In Phase 6 the left front leg prematurely supports the dog. With three legs in the air and one on the ground the dog appears to be running downhill. The right hind foot finally strikes the ground in Phase 7 and in doing so the hind end arches up high and forward because the supporting diagonal front leg is now too close. The space between supporting diagonals at this point should approximate the distance standing.

The judge had many opportunities during the time Bitch B was in the show ring to see her standing naturally. Return from the view going away was an excellent time. In a large class the trick is to retain the true image of the dog standing naturally and relate it to the action you saw in profile because, on a final look down the line, examples like Bitch B can be stacked to produce a much improved final impression.

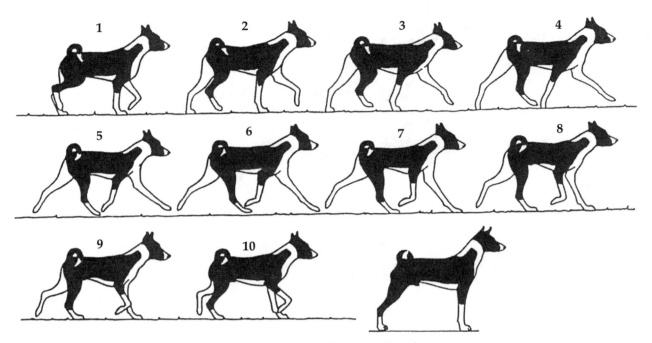

Basenji Illustrated Sequence Dog A

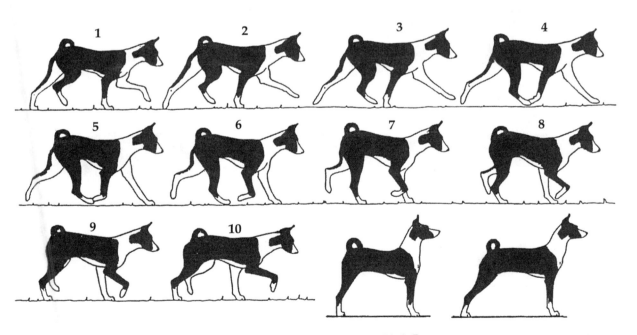

Basenji Illustrated Sequence Bitch B

CHAPTER TWENTY-SEVEN
COLOR MARKING ILLUSIONS

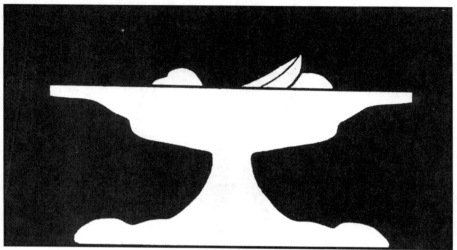

What did you see first?

Which did you see first — the dish of fruit or the two German Shorthaired Pointer heads? Black and white drawings and geometric cubes that spontaneously change in appearance not only have a peculiar fascination but they serve to demonstrate that in the world of dogs things are not always what they seem. This is especially true of canine color marking, and using the Whippet, Great Dane, and Dalmatian as subjects I will attempt to illustrate how unwary judges can be deceived by such markings.

Whippets, A and B

The Whippet

Here are two identical Whippets, a white and a black. They stand the same height but the black appears smaller. In the *Extended Breed Standard of the Whippet*, compiled by Ann Mitchell, the section on color reads in part, "as in many breeds, marking can deceive the eye, sometimes to the dog's benefit, and sometimes not. Black and blues tend to look spindly."

Whippets, C and D

Appearances can be deceiving. C and D are the same dog. This illustration demonstrates how a dark color-marked white dog can be presented to the dog's disadvantage when the exhibitor's clothes are of similar color. Shape, as we all know, can be distorted by various illusions. The visual system encodes objects primarily in terms of their contours, and to the unwary, Dog C appears to have a dip in its back.

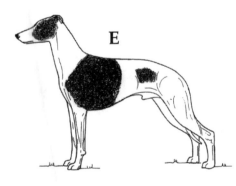

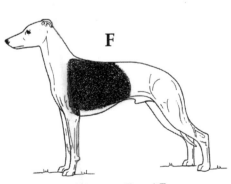

Whippets, E and F

Continuing to use the Whippet as our markings subject, note that Dog E is white above the muzzle, complementing length. His long, well laid-back shoulder blade and upper arm are highlighted by body marking as are the well-sprung ribs. The same body marking lines up the elbow with the deep brisket. The marking at loin suggest shortness.

For Dog F, the vertical marking in front of the shoulder creates an illusion. This pattern makes the shoulder blade and upper arm seem steeper than they are. By color extending to the elbow, yet leaving a portion of the bottom of the chest white, the impression is created that the body is shallow. Absence of color marking on the head doesn't enhance the requirement for a long and lean skull, or improve expression.

Dog G is an almost solid color example in which three white markings create the illusion that the forechest is absent, that the body is shallow, and that the dog lacks underjaw. Solid color heads appear to lack expression (U.K. Extended Standard).

With Dog H, heavy markings carried two-thirds of the way down the foreface makes the muzzle appear shorter than it actually is. The dark stocking on the left foreleg disturbs the eye standing and coming at the trot. The marking on the left hindleg creates the illusion that angulation is lacking at stifle.

The heavy marking extending down the neck of Dog I gives an impression of shortness and thickness to the neck. The marking over the left rump changes the shape of the topline and optically steepens the buttocks, reducing the impression of hindquarter power.

With Dog J, the white around the eyes are left bare by the dark hood marking. This does nothing to enhance the beauty of the head and is distracting; the head appears to lack correct "keen, intelligent, alert expression." The marking on the front leg may confuse the eye when the dog is coming at the trot whereas the marking on the hid leg optically adds to the length of the second thigh, weakens it and produces a crouching outline.

We have seen how the eye can be led by certain markings quite easily. For the judge who does not examine each dog carefully, noting the influence of shape and balance of markings, he can allow the dog's markings to lead to the wrong conclusion, sometimes in the final moments of the decision making. This can work to a dog's favor as well as to its disadvantage. To quote my friend the late Tom Horner in *U.K. Dog World*, 1985, "It is little wonder that there are often disagreements between ringside judges and those in the center of the ring when slight differences in the size and placement of markings can so easily give a false impression about exactly how dogs are put together and balanced."

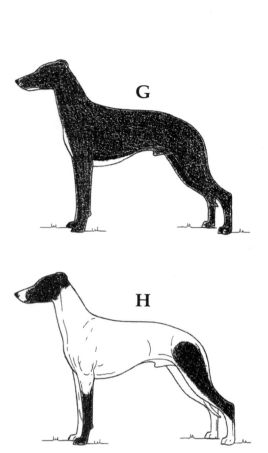

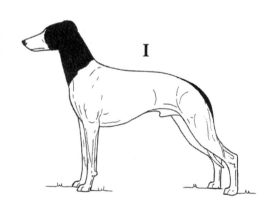

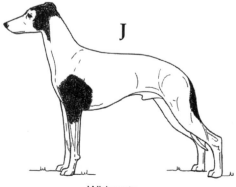

Whippets

Great Danes

The Great Dane

With the exception of color markings, these two Harlequin Great Danes are equal. In the show ring which one of these two Danes should win? The Great Dane Standard advises "a pure white neck is preferred" in Harlequins; therefore Dog A is the winner. Why? It is likely because neck markings can distract and can also create the optical illusion of shortness or heaviness.

The Dalmatian

The open area of white on Dog B below is called a window. In this case it is a round window, a fault in a breed like the Dalmatian where "markings and their overall appearance are very important points to be evaluated." Markings on Dog A are almost perfect but you may have noticed that he is about two inches too long in body. Otherwise they are quite similar.

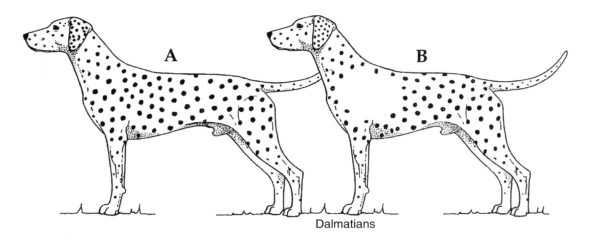

Dalmatians

You have a choice. There is no doubt the round, open window disturbs the eye, more perhaps than Dog A's long body. However the Standard also informs that, "In keeping with the Dalmatian's historical use as a coach dog, gait and endurance are of great importance," and "the overall length of body from the forechest to the buttocks is approximately equal to the height at the withers."

It is at this point in the ring that the judge takes the time to view their off side, the side seldom seen. It is possible that either's opposite side may have masses of black or open areas. On examination it is found that both dogs have correctly spaced and sized spots on their off side. I went with Dog B.

CHAPTER TWENTY-EIGHT
SICKLE HOCKS

The term "sickle hock" is derived from the sickle, a farm tool with a rigid, uncompromising angle where the handle meets the blade. To help illustrate this, I have drawn a dog with his hind leg next to a farmer's sickle. The dog stands with his rear pasterns angled forward from the point of hock to heel pad. At the trot this hock joint doesn't open fully to allow hind leg follow-through to happen. Anyone who has swung a golf club or a baseball bat is aware of the advantage of a follow-through. The follow-through smoothly finalizes the action. The exception in baseball might be a bunt. The exception in dog locomotion is the sickle hock. Sickle hock action is stiff and restricted with almost no use made of the hock joint to aid in forward propulsion. Sometimes a dog will stand sickle hocked, but having a strong Achilles tendon, manages to open the hock at a full trot. More often than not a dog that stands sickled moves in a stilted, uneconomical fashion.

Sickle hock illustrated

The Dachshund

The Dachshund in Illustrated Sequence One on the next page is not sickle hocked. If he were, faulty action would manifest itself in Phase 4, 5 and 6. Instead, the left rear pastern in Phases 5, 6 and 7 extends rearward beyond the perpendicular. Dachshunds, because of their short legs, low-slung body and the tendency for the rear pasterns to lengthen, are prime candidates for sickle hocks.

The poorly constructed Dachshund in Illustrated Sequence Two stands sickle hocked and moves sickle hocked. Each sequence begins with the right front leg in vertical support, the position of the other three legs varies from dog to dog depending on the dog's individual structure. The action phase-by-phase, when compared to the better constructed Dachshund illustrated in Sequence One, shows this dog's sickle hock does not extend rearward beyond the vertical in Phases 4, 5 and 6. Follow-through is almost non-existent. The Dachshund Standard warns of this restricted action in its description of hind leg propulsion, i.e., "The propulsion of the hind leg depends on the dog's ability to carry the hind leg to complete the extension. Viewed in profile the forward reach of the hind leg equals the rear extension." His left rear extension does not equal the forward reach of the right hind leg.

October

Much like the World Series or Super Bowl, the Breeder's Cup Championship in horse racing is also a year-end showcase of the sport's greatest athletes. The championship brings together the world's best horses to compete in eight exciting races, culminating in a multi-million dollar event.

© Bob Langrish

18
Monday

November

Are you overwhelmed by the different kinds of bits, bridles, saddles, and other equipment? Don't worry; there are many books and experts out there to help you make informed choices. Remember, if your equipment fits well and is properly cared for, it should last for many years.

18
Thursday

Dusty L. Perin

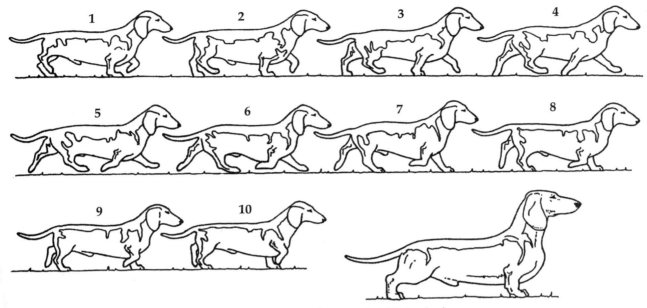

Illustrated Sequence One—not sickle hocked

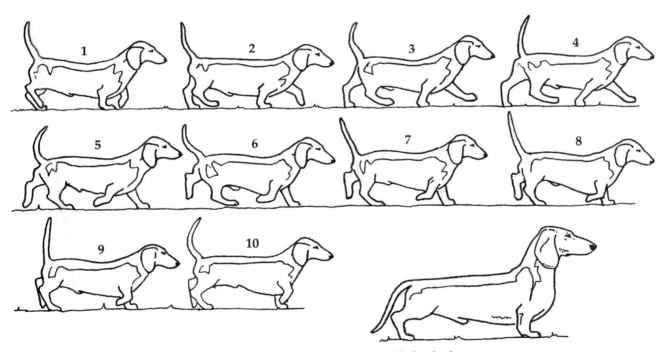

Illustrated Sequence Two—sickle hocked

149

The Wire Fox Terrier

Sickle hocks are a problem in Wire Fox Terriers more frequently than in Smooth Fox Terriers because breeders have bred for a longer second thigh on the Wire. To regain balance, the feet often come forward under the body in the form of a sickle hock, the sickle appearance hidden in part by 1½ inches of wiry hair. In addition, neither Fox Terrier breed extend their hind legs forward and rearward to the same extent as most other breeds. Their legs hang perpendicular and swing parallel to the sides like the pendulum on a clock, the front pasterns flex only slightly as they are brought forward. Balanced with front, the hind leg should extend rearward the same distance as it reaches forward under the body. The sickle hocked Wire in this sequence is unable to extend the hind leg rearward.

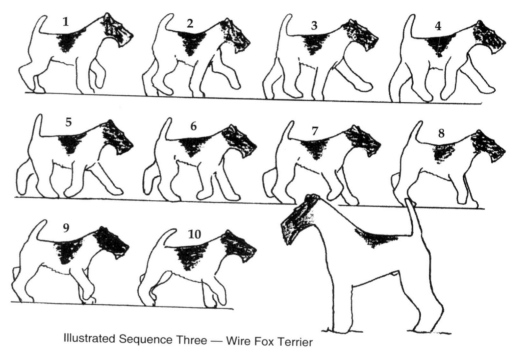

Illustrated Sequence Three — Wire Fox Terrier

The Smooth Fox Terrier

Unlike the Wire, the Smooth Fox Terrier in Sequence Four on the next page was moved on a loose lead. The tight lead on the Wire supported a poor front, the front feet seldom touching the ground. Exhibitors of steep-shouldered Fox Terriers will try to convince you that because this breed is naturally feisty, a tight lead is a must. This well-put-together Smooth Fox Terrier, with all four feet on the ground, serves to illustrate the manner in which I believe this breed should move at the trot. First of all, you can see from his profile stacked that he is neither too long in the leg nor too short—and this is important. Secondly, he has what is called a "Fox Terrier Front" not a Terrier Front. The Fox Terrier Front is almost a straight line down from the point of shoulder to feet allowing for a slight forechest, a slight slope to the correctly short upper arm, and a very slight slope to the front pastern. This kind of front is not conducive to great reach and extension but the reach is there and so is the extension.

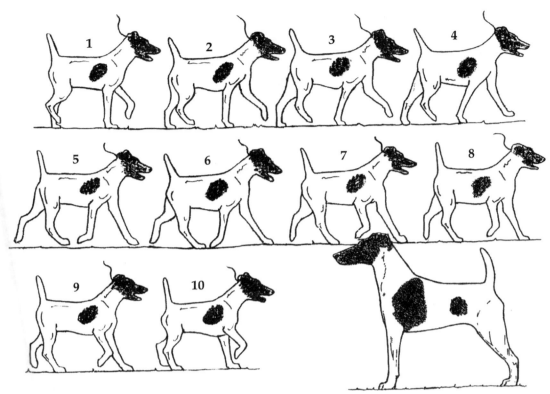

Illustrated Sequence Four — Smooth Fox Terrier

Watch for foot pads on some breeds

Pad Exposure

Several breeds have been brought to my attention as needing to be watched closely to ensure hind leg extension — Pembroke Welsh and Cardigan Welsh Corgis, Schipperkes, Dachshunds, and English Cockers to name a few. In these breeds and many others, we are advised to look for the exposure of rear pads as the dog moves away. One Dachshund breeder writes, "The thrust of correct movement is seen when the rear pads are clearly exposed during rear extension." This is true but not reliable, both the Dachshund and the English Cocker illustrated going away are sickle hocked and their pads can be seen. A dog would have to be very badly sickle hocked not to expose his pads. In Dachshunds they call such a dog a "belly thumper."

Racing Dachshunds

What have sickle hocks to do with this trace of a racing Dachshund? Well, this fast dog was captured on film exhibiting the Sighthound second period of suspension at the gallop, an action reserved for fast Sighthounds and it would seem, fast Dachshunds. Three more Dachshunds in a photograph accompanying an article by Alan Dalton in *The Dachshund Reporter* were captured in similar poses racing at the Cow Palace in San Francisco before an enthusiastic group of 900 people. Subsequently I filmed a number of Dachshunds at the trot and then at the gallop. The effort was rewarded. I found that only the dogs that could extend their rear pasterns beyond the perpendicular were able to stretch forth all four legs forward and back free of contact with the ground, as illustrated here.

A Racing Dachshund

The English Cocker

Now, if you didn't know before, you know something of faulty sickle hocks. Applying this knowledge in the show ring would seem to be a simple matter. For instance, you have this class of three bitches, each with one visible fault. You are invited to place them first, second, third.

English Cockers

Bitch A has a poor head, Bitch B has sickle hocks, and Bitch C is long of body, but otherwise they are almost identical. Where there is a potential for dozens of faults to weigh against virtues these three bitches have only one fault each. Simple? It could be, but unless you have your priorities firmly fixed for each breed at hand, it seldom is! There are breeder judges who have made their placements even before they read this paragraph. Now it is your turn — how would you rank these three; first, second and third? One breeder noted, "I can correct a poor head in one generation. The other faults are more difficult to correct." In my opinion any one of these three bitches could be the winner, depending on the judge; so whatever your placement, you are correct. I would select Bitch A first, Bitch C second and Bitch B third.

English Cockers

Let's look at another group of three. Bitch E is the same as the sickle hocked Bitch B in the previous example except for coat pattern. Could you forgive her sickle hocks and place her first in this class? This time her competitor, Bitch D, in addition to a poor head, has a second visible fault. What is it? Bitch F is also in competition even though she is even longer than the other competitors. The question is — is she too long to consider for first? What about poor-headed Bitch D? Did you determine that her second fault was short legs? Are these departures serious enough to allow sickle hocked Bitch E to place first? Ringside, half of the people are not aware of Bitch E's sickle hocks and the other half do not see it as a big deal. What are you going to do?

What I Would Do

Interesting. It is one of those damned if you do and damned if you don't situations that judges are often confronted with. I have attended a number of English Cocker Specialties here and abroad as well as judging the breed. In almost every instance under Specialists, sickle hocks were easily forgiven. Following the lead of most specialists, I'm willing to forgive the sickle hocks in favor of Bitch E. I placed Bitch F second and Bitch D third.

CHAPTER TWENTY-NINE
SURPRISE BITES

Imagine you are judging the Working Group and are surprised at what you find when you examine the Boxer's mouth. You did not judge the Boxers at the breed level but are aware there were 12 entered. You are impressed with the Best of Breed Boxer's type, balance, soundness and movement as shown in the illustration below. She is contender for first place, however you have belatedly uncovered an issue with the teeth.

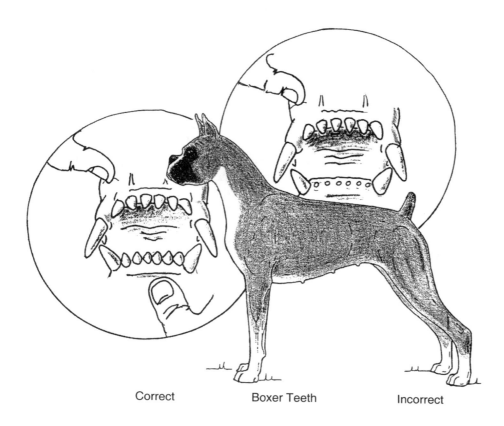

Correct   Boxer Teeth   Incorrect

The Boxer

On examination this Boxer's six lower incisors appall you. The bite shown above right is correct, however each of the six lower incisors is only the size of the head of a half-buried, small, white mapping pin. Viewed head-on with the lips pulled back, you can see in the mouth detailed the six, small, white nubs. The detail to the left is correct for a Boxer bite with large lower incisors in a straight line, and large upper incisors in a slightly convex line.

Surprise! Unless you have previously encountered this situation you are probably as surprised as I was. Until you checked the bite this Boxer was your best in Group. Now what are you going to do? Did the person who judged the classes miss seeing these nubs or was he or she willing to forgive them? Will you be doing the breed a disservice if you award her first? In circumstances like this two more thoughts go through some judges' minds: (1) If I don't give the Boxer first, what will the ringside reaction be to my judging since observers do not know the mouth is incorrect?; and (2) What will be the reaction of the Best-in-Show judge when he opens the mouth? What would you decide?

My Opinion

I did not give this otherwise excellent Boxer first in Group. I could not get past those six tiny white nubs. Since that experience I have had occasion to ask a number of Boxer breeders and judges about this unusual departure. Some claim they are unaware of a problem, others are aware and are concerned. Some said that the gums could be cut back. Some say the problem is genetic, others say it is due to wear. Either way, if you are ever confronted with this departure, it will not come to you as a surprise.

The Upper Teeth

Staying with the Boxer for a moment, I wonder, after seeing numerous bad Boxer bites, if exhibitors really read, comprehend and breed to the Standard's description of the correct Boxer bite. A scissors bite is not correct for the Boxer — note that the canines touch. The Standard advises that the Boxer's bite is undershot, but note the form of undershot seen here where the upper incisors touch the back of the lower incisors. In the correct Boxer bite the upper incisors touch the back of the lower canines which are ideally positioned in line with the incisors, the slightly convex upper line of incisors fitting snugly in back of the lower canine teeth on each side. This form of undershot mouth is difficult to breed for. More often than not the upper teeth are a far cry from fitting snugly back of the lower teeth.

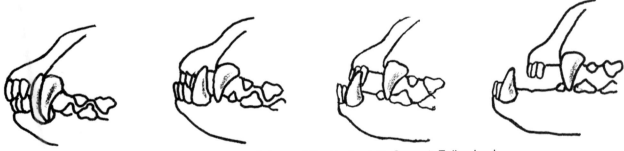

Boxer upper teeth, L to R: Scissors bite, Undershot, Correct, Fallen back

Instead of fitting snugly behind the lower canine teeth, which preferably are positioned up along side the lower incisors, the upper teeth on many Boxers have fallen back an inch or more behind the lower teeth leaving a vast, empty gap. This departure from fitting snugly doesn't, on the surface, appear to bother many breeders, perhaps because the thick upper lip is padded and is able to fill out the space between the two lower canines regardless of where the upper jaw is positioned. If fitting snugly is preferred then the question is how far back can the upper incisors position from the lower canines before the bite is unacceptable?

The Chinese Shar Pei

Enough on Boxer bites. The Chinese Shar Pei shown here has an unusual lower jaw problem one seldom hears about. The problem is called a tight lip, a situation where the lower lip rolls over the six lower incisors and fastens tightly to them. Eventually this departure can produce an overshot bite instead of the desired scissors bite. Judges in the past, unable to find the bite, have been known to assume that the top and bottom incisors have met. They seldom do when tight lip occurs.

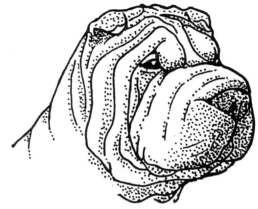

Chinese Shar Pei with jaw problem

I have touched on this unusual departure before, as have others. I thought the authors of the January 12, 1998 revised Standard might warn of this condition as well as attempt to correct the past oversight of not including mention of the lower jaw. In their wisdom they chose not to. Instead they continue to advise, "Deviation from a scissors bite is a major fault."

The Irish Wolfhound

When the Irish Wolfhound Standard was written it contained no mention of the mouth. The people who wrote the Standard 60-odd years ago considered it unnecessary since the Wolfhound was a hunter. It was not necessary to mention so obvious a requirement as a complete, scissors bite. They should have, however, because missing Wolfhound teeth, leaving great gaps, have become common, as shown here.

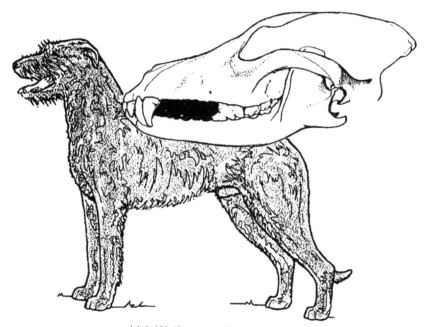

Irish Wolfhound with gap in teeth

Because of this omission, there were exhibitors who believed that if the Standard did not mention teeth then there was no need to open the mouth. The AKC Irish Wolfhound Standard still does not include a requirement for teeth, however thanks to the insistence of judges, the number of teeth in Wolfhound heads have greatly increased. Judges today who are aware of this history make a point of checking for missing Wolfhound teeth.

Japanese Chin exhibiting "wry mouth"

Wry Mouth

Most short-faced breeds are plagued with a condition called wry mouth. Some Standards, like that of the Bichon Frise, warn of wry mouth. Jari Bobillot wrote in the AKC Gazette Japanese Chin Breed Column that many exhibitors seem unaware of this condition and suggests that we focus some serious attention on this problem and eradicate it.

Wry mouth probably originated from "awry," meaning off kilter or crooked. Frank Jackson's *Dictionary of Canine Terms* describes wry mouth as a "lower jaw laterally displaced so that the teeth do not occlude correctly." This departure takes more than one form in addition to degree. These forms are easier for me to depict than describe. One form is where the lower or upper jaw tilts face-on and where the teeth occlude correctly on the dog's right but leaves a gap open on the left side.

Three forms of wry mouth, L to R: Tilts face-on, Occluded, Leaves a gap

As shown in the next two drawings, wry can be so slight as to be unnoticeable (left) or so severe that the dog cannot keep its tongue within its mouth (right). At that stage the dog has difficulty eating and drinking.

Two more examples of wry mouth

The English Toy Spaniel Standard advises, "A wry mouth should be penalized; a hanging tongue is extremely objectionable," whereas a Brussels Griffon with a hanging tongue is disqualified.

English Toy Spaniel, Brussels Griffon

A wry mouth can expose a canine tooth and pull the septum off center. The French Bulldog Standard reads, "flews back, thick and broad meet the under lip in front and cover teeth, which are not seen when the mouth is closed."

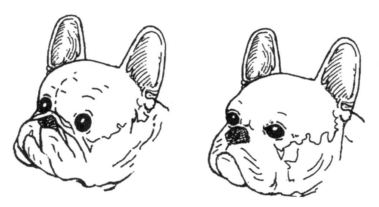

The French Bulldog on the left with wry mouth exposes a canine tooth

The Boston Terrier Standard calls for the chops to completely cover the teeth when mouth is closed and, "Wry mouth is a serious fault."

Correct Boston Terrier head

Premolars and Molars

When molars are missing they are usually premolars, the first four molars on each side of the upper and lower jaw. The small molar closest to the large canine is most likely to be absent. Even when present, as shown here, there is a normal gap between the small first premolar and the large canine. This normal gap filled by the upper canine is, on occasion, mistaken for a missing tooth.

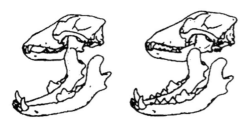

Molars missing (left), molars present (right)

Finding enough space for good-sized molars when the jaws are short is a problem. Because of lack of space the teeth close up. To make room, some turn at right angles while others shrink or disappear. But you have probably never seen that happen, and likely never will. Few undershot breeds are permitted to display their back teeth nor does the exhibitor like having mouths examined to that degree. As for the six front incisors, they are often out of line as shown in the center drawing or, due to a narrow jaw, carry only five incisors as seen on the right.

Molars detailed

Examining Undershot Bites

In some of the Toy breeds, Pekingese and Pugs come first to mind, there is an assumed tradition that it is not really necessary to see the teeth. It is assumed that one can assess the bite without opening the mouth. This is done by feeling the teeth with the mouth closed. I open the mouths of Pekes and Pugs when I judge them to be sure the bite is undershot and the dog has teeth. I do so because Nigel Aubrey Jones, long-time Peke breeder and judge, does. In an article in *Dog News*, Jones advises he has always and still does open the mouths of Pekes when he judges them and mentions that there is a proper way to do so. He goes on to say that without thorough visual inspection he doubts that anyone could be sure a Pekingese is correctly undershot and has a mouthful of teeth in the right place. And, that perhaps not seeing bites may be the reason why we have many Champions in the breed that have such weak underjaws and their teeth have a terrier bite.

Dogs That "Eat Their Heads"

After completing a judging assignment in Melbourne, Australia, I had an opportunity to have an interesting chat with exhibitors of a breed that shall remain nameless. One of the subjects discussed was the concern for a particular mouth problem. The concern was for the comparatively high incidence of dogs "eating their own heads," a problem that occurs when the lower left canine presses against the roof of the dog's mouth, often leaving an indentation in the roof of the mouth.

Later, I began to realize that their breed was not the only breed with this problem. In the show ring I have encountered Rough Collies, Shelties, Bull Terriers, Wire Fox Terriers, Smooth Standard Dachshunds, and Miniature Poodles — to name a few — who are handicapped by this debilitating fault. In many instances the exhibitor was clearly unaware there was a bite problem.

The problem as shown in head A is seldom noticed. Many judges are unaware that there is a problem. In most breeds the judge's attention is focused on ensuring that the upper six incisors overlap the six lower incisors in a scissors bite. When the incisors are correctly positioned the canines receive little attention. Can you see what is wrong?

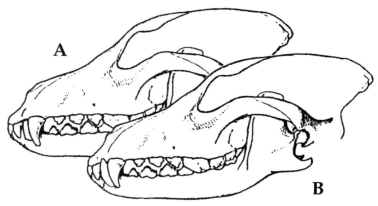

"Dogs that eat their heads" (A) and Normal Bite (B)

What has happened is that the lower left canine, instead of positioning and passing on the outside of the upper jaw as in head B, is inside pressing against the roof of the dog's mouth. This causes a trauma in the soft tissue of the upper jaw. Eventually this dog, when it closes its mouth, will produce an indentation in the roof of the mouth. The cause of this fault is varied. A wry mouth can cause it. A lower jaw that is too narrow or an upper jaw that is too wide can cause it. Insufficient bottom flare outwards of the canines can cause it.

At one show a Sheltie that I thought might compete for Winners had an unusual bite. The owner had found a simple way to save this dog from "eating his own head." The owner had the offending canine removed! This dog, I later found out, only needed a major that day to finish!

Why Look For Correct Bites

The six lower and six upper incisors are used for slicing, the norm being a scissors bite. The correct number and position of incisors is important to the bitch releasing her newborn puppies from the fetal sac. It is the norm for wild dogs that have no human help.

It is not clearly understood what purpose the premolars are designed to serve. Their absence is more readily forgiven than incisors or molars. The molars are used for grinding bones etc. The bitch uses her molars to sever the umbilical cord of her puppies and to crush the ends of the cord to reduce post-natal bleeding.

The importance of a complete and correctly positioned bite varies from breed to breed, but it can be seen that teeth in the dog are more important than other show points such as grooming and the amount of coat carried.

IN CONCLUSION

Having an "eye for a dog" combines both science and art. Knowledge of the science of the dog and the ability to develop an appreciation for the art involved are required for the successful judge and exhibitor. On the science side, you must know the purpose a breed serves. This provides the clues as to how the dog should be structured and move. The art involves the ability to recognize beauty, form, symmetry and style — in other words the dog's aesthetic appeal. One category complements the other. Without the application of science, judging would be poor, and the same can be said for art.

The beauty of developing an eye for a dog is that with more experience, the assessment of a dog will take less time. A judge who has a good eye for a dog has trained himself to take in the appearance of the whole dog at once, almost unconsciously, by summing up each of the parts one by one. The good eye can instantly recognize quality or the lack of it both when the dog is stacked and when it is moving. My hope is that the judging scenarios and illustrations in this book have helped you make progress in developing your eye whether you are a judge, an exhibitor or an avid follower of the sport of showing dogs.

ABOUT THE AUTHOR

Bob with Am-Can Ch. *Charbar's Winter Fashion.*
Breeder, Owner, Handler Barbara Vann. 1992.

Robert W. Cole was a noted international conformation judge, illustrator and author of dozens of articles on purebred dogs. His earlier achievements included illustrating the classic *Dog Locomotion and Gait Analysis* by Curtis Brown, writing and illustrating *The Basenji Stacked and Moving* and authoring the *You Be the Judge* series of breed-specific judging booklets. Bob was a regular columnist for *Dogs in Canada, Dog News, Dog World* (U.K.), *Ilio & Popoki* as well as dog magazines in Australia and New Zealand. Bob lived in Canada with his wife of 50 years, Louise, Bull Terriers and Basenjis.

INDEX

More GREAT dog books from Dogwise Publishing
www.dogwise.com or 800-776-2665, M-F 7:30 am-4:00 pm (Pacific Time)

Dog Friendly Gardens, Garden Friendly Dogs, Smith, 2004, pbk, 188 pgs, #DEG725 $19.95
Combine your love of dogs with love of gardens with the first book ever written that shows you exactly how to design your garden with your dog in mind and train your dog with your garden in mind.

Positive Perspectives: Love Your Dog, Train Your Dog, Miller, 2004, pbk, 258 pgs, #DTB771 $18.95
Transform bad behavior into good behavior with management, consistency, exercise and fun. For the new puppy or second hand dog owner, a complete resource for living with your dog.

Aggression In Dogs: Practical Management, Prevention & Behaviour Modification, Aloff, 2002, pbk, 425 pgs, #DTB755 $49.95   Learn how to solve dog to dog and dog to human aggression problems. Includes detailed protocols for retraining and a complete basic training course.

Behavior Problems in Dogs, 3rd ed., Campbell, 1999, pbk, 328 pgs, #DTB755 $24.95
The reference book your veterinarian has used for years to help solve problem behavior is now available to trainers and pet owners.

Dog Behavior Problems: The Counselor's Handbook, Campbell, 1999, pbk, 115 pgs, #DTB646 $19.95
Learn the people as well as the business side of being a professional dog trainer. How to set rates, manage time and handle sessions.

Dog Language, An Encyclopedia of Canine Behavior, Abrantes, 1997, pbk, 265 pgs, #DTB534 $19.95
Using research with wolves in the wild, this ethologist helps you learn what your dog's body language is telling you. Dozens of illustrations. A-Z format.

Therapy Dogs: Training Your Dog To Reach Others, Diamond-Davis, 2002, pbk, 264 pgs, #DTH121 $19.95
Become a therapy team by training your dog to work with elders, children, and the public in nursing homes, schools and other settings.

Canine Cineradiography Video, Rachel Page Elliott, 45 min., #DAN121 $34.95
Moving x-ray footage of the structure of the dog. Helps in understanding orthopedic problems and injuries.

Dogsteps Video, Rachel Page Elliott, 65 min., #DAN108 $34.95
Companion video to the perennial best-selling book on canine gait and movement, *Dogsteps, A New Look*. A rare look at what is happening inside the dog as the he moves using x-rays. See both correct and incorrect structure in action.

Training Dogs, A Manual, Most, 1954 (reprint), pbk, 204 pgs, #DGT223 $17.95
The book that educated the modern dog trainer. Methods were revolutionary for the time and the foundation for today's training.

Canine Terminology, Spira, 1982 (reprint), hbk, 147 pgs, #DAN120 $24.95
A-Z dictionary of canine terms with detailed illustrations. Every judge, breeder and show person needs this resource.

Evolution of Canine Social Behavior, 2nd ed, Abrantes, 2004, pbk, 96 pgs, #DTB535 $12.95
Learn the scientific basis of domestic dogs' biological relationship to wolves. Understand how it is that we can understand dog behavior by observing wolves.

Mastering Variable Surface Tracking, The Component Tracking, Book & Workbook Set, Presnall, 2004, pbk & spiral, 226 pgs and 130 pgs, #DGT230 $49.95   A detailed program to train your dog for the newest AKC tracking sport. Consists of a training guide and workbook with training maps.

The Dog In Action, Lyon, 1950 (reprint), pbk, 204 pgs, #DAN102 $24.95
One of the first books on structure and movement of the dog. It opened up minds and eyes when it was first published. Still useful today.

New Knowledge of Dog Behavior Pfaffenberger, 1963 (reprint), pbk, 208 pgs, #DTB154 $19.95
The landmark work that established the science of puppy temperament testing and critical periods of socialization and development. For breeders, trainers and owners.

The History and Management of the Mastiff, Baxter and Hoffman, 2004, pbk, 282 pgs, #B1536 $24.95
Learn about the challenges and tragedies that almost made this noble breed extinct. Pedigrees, info on the breed around the world.

Raw Dog Food. Make It Easy for You and Your Dog, MacDonald, 2004, pbk, 86 pgs, #DN208 $12.95
Learn how to prepare a healthy raw food diet for your dog. Easy to follow instructions to mass produce and store this new but old way of feeding dogs.